# PROJECT
## MANAGEMENT
## STRATEGIES OF
# AMERICA

# PROJECT MANAGEMENT STRATEGIES OF AMERICA

THOMAS KIELBASINSKI

**ARPress**

ILLUMINATING IDEAS.
EMPOWERING VOICES

**ARPress**
45 Dan Road Suite 5
Canton MA 02021

Hotline: 1(888) 821-0229
Fax:     1(508) 545-7580


Ordering Information:
Quantity sales. Special discounts are available on quantity purchases by corporations, associations, and others. For details, contact the publisher at the address above.

Printed in the United States of America.

ISBN-13:   Softcover    979-8-89356-386-3
           eBook        979-8-89356-384-9

Library of Congress Control Number: 2024903107

# TABLE OF CONTENTS

# CHAPTER 1

## Belle Vernon Evacuation Project

### Homeland Security

The purpose of this project is to develop a detailed plan for Belle Vernon Homeland Security is coherent and comprehensive to the authorities, which will then be implemented to make the most effectivehomeland security plan. This plan will a on different areas of the town to achieve this purpose effectively.

When researching this subject matter, it is essential to be aware of terms parallel to this matter. Homeland is known as where in whichpeople live and is made up of physical geography, natural resourcesgeography, cultural geography, social geography, and economic geography. Security is defined as the safety of the local, state, and national communities, citizens, and governments. The definition ofrisk assessment and planning are estimating and analyzing certain disasters of the specific location. This assessment and plan determines where an area like Belle Vernon should go with its evacuation process. The definition of mitigation is to reduce the probability of a disaster. Chief of Belle Vernon Police, John Hartman, is the officer responsible for training the residents in Belle Vernon, to be aware of what couldhappen even in a small area. Even though the chances are very slim of any type of an attack on an area the size of Belle Vernon or North Belle Vernon, these training and lookout efforts help make responses faster and recovery less costly. As long as it is a disaster that is within our areaof control, the area can handle it, but if not, the problems could affectmore than just the Belle Vernon area.

Preparedness is to be alert and think ahead about areas like BelleVernon through any type of small disasters and even larger disasters, should they occur. This also puts the federal, state and local governmentsinto action to be better organized for the disaster in smaller areas.

The definition of response is to react to the disaster as soon as possible and is able to relief to the disaster. Response also includes the area in which relief would be provided, response for emergencies and disasters, search and rescue squads for floods, emergency shelters (Schools, and Fire Halls), medical care for the injured, hospitals if possible to reach them, the 5 Red Cross, the Salvation Army, and massfeeding.

Recovery is the ability to return to a level of normality in a givenperiod. The recovery of a town or city depends on the amount of damage, which may be either short term or long term. The short-termprocess would be for disasters such as blizzards, floods, and minor tornadoes. The short-term processes would consist of keeping food and water well stocked, candles, flashlights, and other sources of powerin case the power goes out. The long-term recovery would consist ofperiods of months or years for recovery. After a dead hit by Hurricane Andrew in 1992 in South Florida, it took at least two years to recover. Many citizens can say that the two worst days of their life was after theSalisbury Tornadoes of May 31st and June 2nd, 1998. The clean-up and recovery from these two tornadoes would take them almost a year and a half to recover from such devastation of two F-3 tornadoes. Thesetwo disasters could not be avoided because of "mother nature." If this happens to a small town like Belle Vernon, the most prepared citizens and planners cannot avoid the horrible results. This is why Homeland Security of natural disasters or terrorist problems through evacuation processes has to be well thought out and planned.

# Objective

Maps of Belle Vernon will be created to develop a coherent evacuation plan for this area. These maps will highlight major highways, hospitals, doctor's offices, schools, police stations, and fire departments. These highways and byways will be used to set up a number of routes. One route may be used for emergency vehicles that will be responding to the emergency, and other routes will be used to evacuate the communityout of the Belle Vernon area. All hospitals, fire stations, police stationsand doctor's office will be identified.

Each area will be examined and assessed in order to make sure that the locations identified are easily accessible for emergency vehicles and the community, so that an evacuation may take place in timely and organized manner. Having knowledge of the location of other elements such as water, sewer and power lines are essential in emergency situations.

All medical facilities in the area will need to be assessed so that each facility can be used for the variety of medical needs. In addition, all medical supplies will need to be counted. A plan of how to distribute all supplies will need to be developedto ensure that each medical and shelter receives the correct amount of supplies.

Another area that will need to be addressed when considering possible terrorist attacks is the use of the bridges and the waterways. Secondly, there will need to be checkpoints in place.

# Data Sharing

Data sharing is important because to come up with the best plan for the town of Belle Vernon, experts and other major figures will help provide some data for Fayette and Washington Counties and not justthe town of Belle Vernon, and North Belle Vernon. This plan must contain good facilities, maintenance in planning and information onevery aspect of the town. The dependability of the Internet for of information is critical because not all of the information on the Internetis accurate.

The cost of GIS data sharing varies from place to place. Over 90 percent of Homeland Security data is the total cost of GIS in itself. This cost easily runs into the billions and billions of dollars from the mining industry and large municipalities. With Belle Vernon being so small the cost would be outrageous.

## Emergencies and Disasters (CERT Program)

In Homeland Security of Pennsylvania, there is a program thatwould greatly benefit the small community of Belle Vernon. This program is called Community Emergency Response Team or CERT. CERT was developed in Los Angeles, CA by the Los Angeles Fire Department in 1985. These CERT programs have been developed in 45 states and 340 communities, which shows that the idea is spreading.

There is a training program for Belle Vernon citizens, if interested in 20 hours during a 7-day week period. These meetings cover firedisasters, medical rescue purposes and body of water rescues. This program is being to be further developed and implemented with over 400,000 volunteers in 56 states and countries throughout the world.

## Emergencies and Disasters (Terrorism)

The definition of Terrorism is violent acts against a nation, country, and state that include intimidation and ransom. These terrorist or evil organizations make people of their government feel hopeless and worthless to fight against these acts.

The threats of violence are very slim for a community like Belle Vernon, but the Chief of Police in Belle Vernon has tried to make citizens aware of the different threats of terrorism, which include: assassinations, kidnappings, hijackings, bomb scares, and cyber-attacks. The training program involved with Chief John Hartman includes the threatening of any of these actions in the Belle Vernon area. For example, the chief of police got a complaint of us college students taking pictures of bridges, buildings, infrastructures, and complexes. This was a major concern in a small community because since 9-11 everyone has been on high alert even in the smaller areas of the country.

Some of the issues that Chief John Hartman keeps his community aware of are: always be aware of the communities surroundings, report all suspicious activity, always to evacuate the closest emergency exit in buildings, and keep first aid a kit handy for medical treatment in your home and on your job, for yourself and others.

There is also a different type of terrorism called cyber-attacks. These cyber-attacks can happen in three different ways: through wires, phone lines, and party access systems. These cyber-attacks can affect the following: ATM machines, computer data, intercept telephone call conversations, and trusted party access system. There is a general evacuation method through homeless shelters when harmful materials are released in restricted areas.

## Preparing and Responding in Building Explosions

The proper methods to prepare and respond are to review evacuation emergency methods and know your direction around your place of work or apartment you rent. Another factor is to know where emergency equipment is, in case of a small fire in hallways or downstairs or in offices. Secondly, then get CPR training or first aid education just in case someone is in need of immediate help. The following thingsare a must for owners of buildings and complexes: portable batteries,flashlights, first aid equipment, and specialized tape to mark dangerouszones and locations.

# Bomb Threats

For people of Belle Vernon, if you receive a bomb threat get as much information as possible from the bomber as quickly as possible and report it to the police. Be very aware of the follow things: unfamiliar packages, letters and gifts sent to you because they could be bomb type devices.

# Biological

The following are specific biological dangers that could cause viruses and diseases through any type of unfamiliar bacteria, viruses, and toxins. The causes of many deaths are through air pollution. Some other dangers are spread through animals and insects such as mice, flies, and mosquitoes. Because some chemicals are sprayed over vegetables and certain types of feeds are given to cattle; food and water contamination can be avoided by making sure that all food is cooked to the maximum and that all meat is cooked till completely done. An example of biological terrorist attacks happened in the fall of 2001, when Anthrax was sent to different government offices and agencies through the mail. This deadly white powder disrupted the mail and other important activities.

A major reason to make people more aware of terrorist threats in certain areas is so the nation as a whole can be more prepared if something like 9-11 should happen again. This is also making smaller communities aware that it doesn't necessarily have to hit the bigger cities for it to be a major disaster. The country also wants its citizens to feel as safe and secure as they were before 9-11.

When it comes to decontamination, there are some things that you should do way to make sure that you don't become contaminated or contaminate someone else. Keep these following things in mind when worried about contamination: Remove all possible contaminated clothing, flush eyes out with non-contaminated water, wash and rinse face with soap and water, and go to the closest hospital for medical checkup.

# Nuclear and Radioactivity Threats

The Nuclear bomb has only been used by the United States against Japan in August of 1945 twice. There have been threats by U.S., Russia, and Iraq from the Cold War Era 1945-1990 and Gulf War Era 1991-1992, but none of these threats have been followed through because the nuclear bomb is 100 times dangerous than a grenade. The Radioactive bomb or "dirty bomb" is more likely to be used in attacks in terrorism because they are easier and less expensive to get. There are several potential targets that terrorists aim for: missile bases, federal government locations, subways, bus stations, manufacturing businesses, and other important businesses. These are also potential targets for Belle Vernon residents, citizens and planners to watch out for, so this is why Chief John Hartman teaches and trains his citizens and fellow officers of the community 24/7. Without the training this will not save lives if it were to happen into community of Belle Vernon. The three keys of protection are shielding, distance and time. The shielding method is good because the thicker in material of the facility you evacuate to the better. This would include bricklayer buildings and steel structures. The distance method is better in places like bathrooms, basements and offices where you are more likely to evacuate to a safer place.

Time is the most critical because you need to evacuate to a safe location as quickly as possible.

# Protective Measures and Threats

There is always a possibility of terrorist's attacks and violence. There are several different conditions or levels of terrorists' attacks. These conditions are low, elevated, guarded and severe. The government goes through proper measures to make sure everyone involved gets the feel for the Homeland Security Advisory System and well-prepared protective measures for the possibility of raising the terrorism threat.

# Belle Vernon/North Belle Vernon Emergency Evacuation Plan:

The purpose of this Evacuation Plan is to develop a plan for the boroughs of Belle Vernon and North Belle Vernon so that during a time of disaster the residents, workers, and community members can be evacuated in an organized manner to maintain the highest level of safety. The map indicates that there are two areas, one of these areas will be Belle Vernon and the other will be North Belle Vernon. The following guidelines and evacuation routes are to be followed in a time of disaster.

Primary Evacuation Zone: The Primary Evacuation Zone is the area that the citizens of the Belle Vernon and North Belle Vernon boroughs would be evacuated to in the event of a terrorist attack. The Primary Evacuation Zone would be in effect if Belle Vernon and/or North Belle Vernon were threatened from the areas along the river, Interstate 70 and/ or the Belle Vernon Bridge.

Secondary Evacuation Zone: The Secondary Evacuation Zone is the area that the citizens of the Belle Vernon and North Belle Vernon Boroughs would be evacuated to in the event of a terrorist attack. The Secondary Evacuation Zone would be in effect if Belle Vernon and/or North Belle Vernon were threatened from the areas along the Central Business District and Rostraver Shopping Plaza.

Section A: In the case of the Primary Evacuation Zone: All citizens within Belle Vernon area in Fayette County would drive west on Route 906 onto State Street, continue up Broad Street toward Rostraver Shopping Plaza. Proceed to the vacant facility that once housed the Ames 13 Department Store. Overflow can proceed to the former Supervalu distribution center. All citizens in the North Belle Vernon area in Westmoreland County should also proceed to the same areas. All churches along the main roads can also be used for overflow. Doctor's offices can only be used for immediate medical attention.

Section B: In case of the Secondary Evacuation Zone: All citizens withthe Belle Vernon area in Fayette County will proceed on Route 906 along the river in the churches and the Maccabee Industrial Inc. facility. If necessary, some overflow can proceed to the municipal building and the Fire Department. All citizens in the North Belle Vernon area in Westmoreland County will proceed down Broad Street to State andonto Route 906 to the same evacuation points. As stated in Section A, other churches that are not affected can also be used for overflow, and Doctor's offices are only to be used for immediate medical attention.

All vehicles must still comply with standard procedures unless otherwise told by safety officials. All traffic trying to proceed in the other direction will not be permitted. There will be no "cross town" traffic unless absolutely necessary. You must drive by the designated routes or as directed by safety officials.

Only Emergency Response vehicles can proceed in any direction other than the ones given. If you are close enough to walk, please do not drive. It will cut downon traffic.

If possible, the Red Cross will be available to help in any way possible. If Mon Valley Hospital, in Charleroi is not accessible, the Jefferson Hospital on Route 51 will be the other alternative. UPMC McKeesport will also be an alternative.

**Some safety concepts to keep in mind:**
- Know your buildings emergency procedures. They are critical to your safety!
- Always remain calm in any emergency.
- If an evacuation is ordered, use the pre-designed route for leavingthe area or the Central Business District.
- If you cannot use the pre-designed route, heed all safety instructionsand follow the general flow of traffic.
- Pre-plan with family members how each will get home in the event of an evacuation.

Plan and discuss secondary access numbers and meeting locations with family members in the event that you unable to contact each other using normal methods.

## History of Belle Vernon

Forty miles south of the city of Pittsburgh lay Belle Vernon Borough, which is nestled on the east bank of the Monongahela River. Belle Vernon is one of the oldest communities along the Monongahela River. As originally plotted, in the 1800's, the town contained 360 lots. Someof them were in Westmoreland County, but most of Belle Vernon isactually in Fayette County.

Because of Belle Vernon's location, it as well as other small cities in the Mon Valley has been known for such businesses as lumbering,boating building and many forms of manufacturing take place. It istold that this area was once inhibited by Indians, wild animals filledthe land, and fish where a common sight in the river. This all changed when settlers moved into this area in the late 1700's.

According to the history of Fayette and Westmorland Counties, a man known as Noah Speers drew up what we know as the very first comprehensive plan for Belle Vernon around 1813. Noah's father was reasonable for buying land in Monongahela, and expanding to where Belle Vernon rests today. The streets of Belle Vernon in the 1800's were as follows: Water, Main, Solomon, Wood, Market, First, Second, Third,and Fourth. The alleys were as follows: Long, Pleasant, Strawberry and Flint.

The first sale of land that took place was on April 18, 1814 and was purchased for ten dollars. A man by the name of Thomas Ward, who was a carpenter, purchased the land and built a house there. This house is known occupied by James Lewis. As more and more people moved into Belle Vernon, so did more businesses. In 1833 Solomon Speers and Morgan Gaskill built 16 the first steamboat to be constructed in Belle

Vernon. Then Henry Speer put a ferry in place along the Monongahela River.

Belle Vernon flourished with more development and William Eberhard founded a glass manufacturing industry in 1836. This glass manufacturing industry was one of the major and chief businesses in Belle Vernon. Manufacturing provided many jobs to residents at that time. As Belle Vernon developed due to manufacturing so did the town itself.

## History of North Belle Vernon

North Belle Vernon celebrated its 128th year as a Borough in February. The town site was laid out in April 1872 but was not incorporated as a Borough until February 28, 1876. The founder was a farmer and a sand dealer by the name of Louis M. Speer. The first election was held in May 1876. W. R. Springer was our first Burgess, which is also known as a representative of a borough. Other council members chosen in 1876 were Peter Corwin, Thomas Hunt, John S.Henry, J.C. Hasson and Francis Keistler. Elected school directors were Thomas Hunt, William Jones, Francis Keistler, J.A. Piersoll, and John S. Henry. The first council meeting was on June 2, 1876 at which Henry was President; Hasson, Secretary; Hunt as Treasurer; and Peter Corwin, Street commissioner. The first Borough tax was 1 1/2 mills, levied on July 27, 1876.

Samuel Dougherty, a carpenter, is claimed to have built the first dwelling in the new Borough on Broad Avenue. He was a very influential person in North Belle Vernon and served in the offices of Justice of the Peace, Council Member, School Director, and Judge of Election, all at the same time. His carpenter shop was also the temporary school. The first two industries in the town were a Foundry in 1873 on Broad Avenue above and a Flour Mill on Speer Street in 1874. Lots were not sold until 1900 and this is when the area really started to build up.

The population was 435 in 1890 and by 1910 it grew to 1520. The 1960 census showed 3,184 residents, followed by 2,916 in 1970, 2,245 in 1980, and 2,112 in 1990, and the most recent count in 2000 was 2,107.

North Belle Vernon has a very good business base with an estimated figure of approximately 100 retailers. We have moderate business baseof approximately one hundred merchants.

North Belle Vernon is one town that can boast of one of the most modern fire departments with the latest equipment, all of which was purchased by funds raised by the department. The fire department celebrated its 100th anniversary in 1995. Police Chief James D. Bedsworth heads the present force of eight officers who provide twenty-four-hour protection to North Belle Vernon. The borough is currently trying to replace all the sanitary sewers.

Along with the modern Fire Department, North Belle Vernon'slibrary is also a facility that is supported and maintained by the residents. The residents take pride in the fact they are willing to keep things moving in their small but progressive town. Public school children attend classes at Belle Vernon Area School District sites located in adjacent Washington and Rostraver Townships. Our one private school, Saint Sebastian, currently has 250 students from preschool to gradeeight

## Current Conditions in Belle Vernon:

Route 88 is a heavily traveled roadway in the Mid Mon Valley region. This roadway may have the potential to become a major commercialroad and there is still some development along the road even thoughthere are the other major interstates in the area.

The North Belle Vernon area is also trying to come up with a new economic strategy. Any economic strategy should address the following elements:

- Identifying sites needing improved infrastructure and access;
- Identifying opportunities and developing recommendations for retrofitting,
- Buildings and sites to current standards,
- Conducting an analysis of vacant space with strategies on how to market the space to progressive, but complimentary firms,
- Suggesting standards for lighting, signage and streetscape improvements that will create a unified visual appeal for new development,
- Defining the obstacles that are located in this central business district, which might hinder business growth (i.e., zoning, lack of infrastructure),
- Identifying traffic and parking issues,
- Determining what types of public investment are needed to assist in this process,
- Identifying the issues that could be of concern to local business owners such as public safety, lack of space, lack of a business organization, perceptions, community identity and proper mix of business types.

## Economic Development

The Washington County Council on Economic Development is a private non-profit located in Washington, PA, the county seat. This organization offers technical assistance, financing and education to businesses located in Washington, Greene, Fayette and Westmoreland Counties. The Mon Valley Progress Council is located in Monessen, Westmoreland County that has the goal to revitalize the economy of the Mid Monongahela Valley through industrial development. The Mon Valley Progress Council has been a leader in supporting the development and construction of the Mon Fayette Expressway.

A workforce development strategy must be created that addresses what types of industries / businesses are needed to support the region in the future. Public policies must then be implemented that will support the development strategy and work to bring about economic growth.

One goal of the economic development strategy should be to establish industry business clusters within the Mid Mon Valley Region. The objective of an industry is to support local businesses and increase the economic vitality of the region. Often industry strategies are implemented to solve crises such as high unemployment rates, recession, stagnant economy, real estate collapse, or loss of key industries. An industry is an interconnected group of firms and industries within a region that conduct business with one another and or share a common need for talent, technology, and infrastructure. The firms and industries may be competitive with other members in the cluster and or they may cooperate with other members.

The Mid Mon Valley Planning and Zoning Commission and local elected officials should initiate networking efforts and planning sessions; ensuring economic development is undertaken through a regional approach. Steps should be taken to open communication and foster relationships with existing business and industry leaders, California University of Pennsylvania, Mon Valley Regional Chamber of Commerce, and Washington County Chamber of Commerce and other local chambers or economic development organizations. Sustainable development is an important issue where businesses and elected officials must consider their relationship and obligation to the community or region in which they are located. These officials should take into consideration the economic, environmental, and social sustainability of their development efforts. Businesses in the region today will need to focus on minimizing the wasteful use of their resources, along with equity and community well-being. A strong regional approach to economic development will be essential and a well thought out zoning ordinance can achieve land use goals to foster and support economic growth.

## Business Located in Belle Vernon

Kelly's Car Wash California Boat ClubMorgovich Signs Darby's
Roscoe Ledger

Spee-D Mart & Sunoco Gas StationJustine's Personal Care Home
Furniture Restoration

White Barn Restaurant

Trisha's Paws & ClawsJohnny's Market Uptown Saloon Walker
Landscaping Lagerheads

Adult Assisted LivingKim T's Ball

Busters R & R Builders

Rotheram Plumbing, Heating, and CoolingKelly Incorporated
Garret Insurance AgencyHighway Appliance

Flo's Personal Home CareLoskos Auto

Fox's Pizza

Mon Valley Community Credit UnionCMM Associates

Storage Building Route 88 Auto Sales

Creative Designs & ExpressionsMelenyzer Funeral Homes Inc.

Hardhat Saloon

Auto Repair

Braun's Bakery Outlet Patricia Roberts Hair SalonRoscoe Laundry

C.L. ElectronicsJay's Tavern

J & J Transmissions

Charlie Roberts Auto RepairCentral Apartments Bradish's Marina

Dunlevy Diving CenterCadillac Joes

McIntosh Masonry & Excavating

Mariner's Hall Dentist Office

Stile Investments & Tax ProfessionalsZanardini Water Service

Bonn Paralegal and Tax ServiceRosko's Bar

Union CleanersD & S Variety Caul's Garage

Annette's Beauty Salon Cupari Home Improvement

# Churches in Belle Vernon

ANTIOCH BAPTIST CHURCH, 412-929-3044 942 HENRY STREET, BELLE VERNON PA 15012

FIRST BAPTIST CHURCH, 412-929-6968 511SHORT STREET, BELLE VERNON PA 15012

OLIVE BRANCH BAPTIST CHURCH, 412-929-2466RURAL ROUTE 3, BELLE VERNON PA 15012

SALEM BAPTIST CHURCH, 412-379-7702 RURAL ROUTE 4, BELLE VERNON PA 15012

PEOPLES BIBLE CHURCH, 412-929-5402 1101HENRY STREET, BELLE VERNON PA 15012

SAINT SEBASTIAN'S CHURCH, 412-929-9300 801 BROAD AVENUE, BELLE VERNON PA 15012

COVENANT CHRISTIAN CHURCH, 412-929-937336 MAIN STREET, BELLE VERNON PA 15012

FIRST CHRISTIAN CHURCH, 412-929-2441 320 MAIN STREET, BELLE VERNON PA 15012

LYNNWOOD LUTHERAN CHURCH, 412-929-4760 900 WASHINGTON ROAD, BELLE VERNON PA 15012

FELLS UNITED METHODIST CHURCH, 412-379-4502 RURAL ROUTE 1, BELLE VERNON PA 15012

FIRST UNITED METHODIST CHURCH, 412-929-4696 200

STATE STREET, BELLE VERNON PA 15012

CHURCH OF THE NAZARENE, 412-929-7196 112 REED
AVENUE, BELLE VERNON PA 15012

FIRST PRESBYTERIAN CHURCH, 412-929-7616 01 FAYETTE
AVENUE, BELLE VERNON PA 15012

MARION PRESBYTERIAN CHURCH, 412-929-738007 PERRY
AVENUE, BELLE VERNON PA 15012
REHOBOTH PRESBYTERIAN CHURCH, 412-929-7020
RURAL ROUTE 3, BELLE VERNON PA 15012

# Hospitals & Airports

## Hospitals/medical centers near Belle Vernon:

MONONGAHELA VALLEY HOSPITAL INC (about 7 miles;
MONONGAHELA, PA)

BROWNSVILLE GENERAL HOSPITAL (about 8 miles;
BROWNSVILLE, PA)

UPMC MCKEESPORT HOSPITAL (about 15 miles;
MCKEESPORT, PA)

## Airports certified for carrier operationsnearest to Belle Vernon:

ALLEGHENY COUNTY (about 16 miles; PITTSBURGH,
PA;ID: AGC)

ARNOLD PALMER REGIONAL (about 34 miles; LATROBE, PA;

ID: LBE)

MORGANTOWN MUNI-WALTER L. BILL HART FLD (about 34miles; MORGANTOWN, WV; ID: MGW)

Other public-use airports nearest to Belle Vernon:

ROSTRAVER (about 7 miles; MONONGAHELA, PA; ID: FWQ)

FINLEYVILLE AIRPARK (about 12 miles; FINLEYVILLE, PA;ID: G05)

BANDEL (about 15 miles; EIGHTY FOUR, PA; ID: 22D)

Colleges/Universities, Public/Private Schools, & Library

**Colleges/Universities with over 2000students nearest to Belle Vernon:**

CALIFORNIA UNIVERSITY OF PENNSYLVANIA (about 5 miles; CALIFORNIA, PA; Full-time enrollment: 5,183)

WESTMORELAND COUNTY COMMUNITY COLLEGE (about 22 miles; YOUNGWOOD, PA; FT enrollment: 3,223)

CARNEGIE    MELLON    UNIVERSITY    (about    23 miles; PITTSBURGH, PA; FT enrollment: 7,903)

ART INSTITUTE PITTSBURGH (about 24 miles; PITTSBURGH, PA; FT enrollment: 2,246)

POINT PARK COLLEGE (about 24 miles; PITTSBURGH, PA; FT enrollment: 2,189)

UNIVERSITY OF PITTSBURGH-MAIN CAMPUS (about 24 miles; PITTSBURGH, PA; FT enrollment: 22,930)

DUQUESNE UNIVERSITY (about 24 miles; PITTSBURGH, PA; FT enrollment: 8,199)

**Public high school in Belle Vernon**

BELLE VERNON AREA HS (Students: 910; Grades: 09 - 12)

Public primary/middle schools in Belle Vernon

ROSTRAVER ELEMENTARY SCHOOL (Students: 671; Grades: KG - 05)

MARION EL SCHOOL (Students: 668; Grades: KG - 05)

BELLMAR MS (Students: 377; Grades: 06 - 08)

ROSTRAVER MS (Students: 350; Grades: 06 - 08)
**Private primary/middle school in Belle Vernon**

BELLE VERNON PUBLIC LIBRARY (Operating income: $42,721; Location: 505 SPEER ST; 21,339 books; 110 audio materials; 229 video materials; 17 serial subscriptions)

# Radio & Television Stations

Strongest AM radio stations in Belle Vernon
WASP (1130 AM; daytime; 5 kW; BROWNSVILLE,PA; Owner: KEYMARKET LICENSES, LLC) WFGI (940 AM; 0 kW; CHARLEROI, PA;

Owner: KEYMARKET LICENSES, LLC)

KDKA (1020 AM; 50 kW; PITTSBURGH, PA; Owner:INFINITY
BROADCASTING OPERATIONS, INC.) WWNL (1080 AM;
50 kW; PITTSBURGH, PA; Owner: STEEL CITY RADIO,
INC.)

WKHB (620 AM; 6 kW; IRWIN, PA; Owner:BROADCAST
COMMUNICATIONS, INC.)

WPTT (1360 AM; 5 kW; MCKEESPORT, PA; Owner: RENDA
BROADCASTING CORPORATION OF NEVADA)

WWCS (540 AM; 5 kW; CANONSBURG, PA; Owner:BIRACH
BROADCASTING CORPORATION) WJAS (1320 AM; 6 kW;
PITTSBURGH, PA; Owner: RENDA BROADCASTING CORP.
OF NEVADA)

WEAE (1250 AM; 5 kW; PITTSBURGH, PA; Owner: ABC,
INC.)WPIT (730 AM; 5 kW; PITTSBURGH, PA; Owner:
PENNSYLVANIA MEDIA ASSOCIATES, INC.)

WWVA (1170 AM; 53 kW; WHEELING, WV; Owner:CAPSTAR
TX LIMITED PARTNERSHIP) WBGG (970 AM; 5 kW;
PITTSBURGH, PA; Owner: AM/FM RADIO LICENSES,
L.L.C.) WPGR (1510 AM; 5 kW; MONROEVILLE,
PA; Owner: MCL/ MCM- INC.)

**Strongest FM radio stations in Belle Vernon**

WOGI (98.3 FM; DUQUESNE, PA; Owner:KEYMARKET
LICENSES, LLC)

WOGG (94.9 FM; OLIVER, PA; Owner:KEYMARKET
LICENSES, LLC)

WVCS (91.9 FM; CALIFORNIA, PA; Owner:FOREVER OF
SOMERSET, INC.)

WVPM (90.9 FM; MORGANTOWN, WV; Owner: WEST
VIRGINIA EDUCATIONAL BROADCASTING AUTHORITY)
WSHH (99.7 FM; PITTSBURGH, PA; Owner:
RENDA B/CING CORP. OF NEVADA) WZPT (100.7 FM;
NEW KENSINGTON, PA; Owner:

INFINITY RADIO SUBSIDIARY OPERATIONS INC.)WRIJ
(106.9 FM; MASONTOWN, PA;
Owner: HE'S ALIVE INC.)

WDSY-FM (107.9 FM; PITTSBURGH, PA; Owner: INFINITY
RADIO SUBSIDIARY OPERATIONS INC.)WJJJ (104.7 FM;
PITTSBURGH, PA; Owner:
CAPSTAR TX LIMITED PARTNERSHIP)

WWSW-FM (94.5 FM; PITTSBURGH, PA; Owner:AM/FM
RADIO LICENSES, L.L.C.)

WLTJ (92.9 FM; PITTSBURGH, PA; Owner: WPNT, INC.)
WLSW (103.9 FM; SCOTTDALE, PA;
Owner: L. STANLEY WALL) WQED-FM (89.3 FM;
PITTSBURGH, PA;
Owner: WQED MULTIMEDIA) WDVE (102.5 FM;
PITTSBURGH, PA; Owner:
CAPSTAR TX LIMITED PARTNERSHIP) WKST-FM (96.1
FM; PITTSBURGH, PA; Owner:CAPSTAR TX LIMITED
PARTNERSHIP)

WRRK (96.9 FM; BRADDOCK, PA; Owner: WPNT INC)
WSSZ (107.1 FM; GREENSBURG, PA; Owner: MCL/MCM-
INC.)

WANB-FM (103.1 FM; WAYNESBURG, PA; Owner:
BROADCAST COMMUNICATIONS, INC.)

WBZZ (93.7 FM; PITTSBURGH, PA; Owner: INFINITY
RADIO SUBSIDIARY OPERATIONS INC.)

WDUQ (90.5 FM; PITTSBURGH, PA;Owner: DUQUESNE
UNIVERSITY)

## TV broadcast stations around Belle Vernon

W26AV (Channel 26; CHARLEROI, PA;Owner: DEBRA
GOODWORTH)
WPCB-TV (Channel 40; GREENSBURG, PA; Owner:
CORNERSTONE TELEVISION, INC.) WQEX (Channel 16;

PITTSBURGH, PA;
Owner: WQED  MULTIMEDIA) W65CG (Channel 65;
PITTSBURGH, PA; Owner:
TRINITY BROADCASTING NETWORK)WPXI (Channel 11;
PITTSBURGH, PA; Owner: WPXI-TV HOLDINGS, INC.)
WTAE-TV (Channel 4; PITTSBURGH, PA; Owner:WTAE
HEARST-ARGYLE TV, INC. (CA CORP.)) WPTG-LP (Channel
69; PITTSBURGH, PA; Owner: ABACUS TELEVISION)
WBGN-LP (Channel 59; PITTSBURGH, PA; Owner:BRUNO
GOODWORTH NETWORK, INC.) WCWB (Channel 22;
PITTSBURGH, PA;
Owner: WCWB LICENSEE, LLC) KDKA-TV  (Channel  2;
PITTSBURGH,  PA;
Owner: CBS BROADCASTING INC.) WPGH-TV (Channel 53;
PITTSBURGH, PA;Owner: WPGH LICENSEE, LLC)
WQED (Channel 13; PITTSBURGH, PA;Owner: WQED
MULTIMEDIA)
WBPA-LP (Channel 29; PITTSBURGH, PA; Owner:VENTURE
TECHNOLOGIES GROUP, LLC) W61CC (Channel 61;
PITTSBURGH, PA;
Owner: THE VIDEOHOUSE, INC.) WIIC-LP (Channel 29;
PITTSBURGH, PA;Owner: ABACUS TELEVISION)
W63AU (Channel 63; PITTSBURGH, PA; Owner:THE BON-
TELE NETWORK, INC.)

WBYD-CA (Channel 35; JOHNSTOWN,PA; Owner:
BENJAMIN PEREZ)
WNPB-TV (Channel 24; MORGANTOWN, WV; Owner:
WESTVIRGINIA EDUCATIONAL BROADCASTING
AUTHORITY)

# Housing

Houses: 720 (612 occupied: 349 owneroccupied, 263 renter occupied)

Rooms in owner-occupied houses in Belle Vernon, Pennsylvania:
1 room: 0
2 rooms: 0
3 rooms: 0
4 rooms: 29
5 rooms: 72
6 rooms: 104
7 rooms: 58
8 rooms: 10
9 or more rooms: 76

Rooms in renter-occupied housing units and apartments:
1 room: 9
2 rooms: 28
3 rooms: 93
4 rooms: 56
5 rooms: 62
6 rooms: 5
7 rooms: 0
8 rooms: 10
9 or more rooms: 0

Year house built:
1999 to March 2000: 35
1995 to 1998: 19
1990 to 1994: 16
1980 to 1989: 9
1970 to 1979: 101

1960 to 1969: 5

1950 to 1959: 64

1940 to 1949: 117

1939 or earlier: 354

Bedrooms in owner-occupied houses in Belle Vernon:

No bedroom: 0

1 bedrooms: 0

2 bedrooms: 110

3 bedrooms: 166

4 bedrooms: 65

5 or more bedrooms: 8

Bedrooms in renter-occupied apartments and housing units:

No bedroom: 9

1 bedroom: 130

2 bedroom: 130

3 bedrooms: 32

4 bedrooms: 0

5 or more bedrooms: 0

## Household type by relationship:

Households: 1177

**In family households:** 851 (217 male householders, 74 female householders) 225 spouses, 277 children (259 natural, 0 adopted, 18 stepchildren), 24 grandchildren, 17 brothers or sisters, 17 parents, 0 other relatives, 0 non-relatives

**In non-family households:** 326 (85 male householders (72 living alone)), (217 female householders (198 living alone)), 24 non-relativesIn group quarters: 14 (0 institutionalized population)

**Size of family households:** 146 2-persons, 66 3-persons, 51 4-persons, 13 5-persons, 7 6-persons, 8 7-or-more-persons

**Size of non-family households:** 270 1-person, 32 2-persons, 0

3-persons, 0 4-persons, 0 5- persons, 0 6-persons, 0 7-or-more-persons

## Role of the Professional Planner

When developing an Evacuation plan for the area of Belle Vernon our group has taken on the role of professional planners. The following is a list of the information and the stages that will need to be followed.

- Gather background data Analyze and interpret the data
- Communicate that data to the planning body and public Organize and present information to the proper authority Compile information and feedback from the presentation Develop alternative plans
- Develop appropriate plans, policy, and producers.
- Plan accessible and coherent documents to the proper authority or public.Put in to place.


Information on the Professional Planner comes from:

Becker, B & Kelley, E. (2000). Community Planning: AnIntroduction to the Comprehensive Plan. Island Press, Washington D.C.Washington Co. Redevelopment Authority, 2002-2003, Washington Chamber of Commerce, 2002.

# CHAPTER 2

## Urban Planning of Somerset County

### Introduction

This project will give you an overview of urban plan of the overall area of Somerset County through history of employment, economic development, annual income, census, places of interest for economic purposes. This project will include statistics in charts, graphs and maps to give a better idea of what Somerset County in comparison with the state of Pennsylvania have for their economic purposes. There will be problems of the economy in this region that will have a solution.

### History of Somerset County

Well before the time of ancestry, there were three Indian tribes in Somerset County that were the Shawnee, Iroquois and Delaware along the Southern Trail. This trail later would be call Route 40. During this time, there was also a northern trail called Forbes Road. Forbes Road was later changed to Route 30. There first city and township to ever be found in this area was Quemahoning Township with the city named Kickenapauling's Town.

http://www.somersetcntypachamber.org/galleries/history/history-1.HTM

By the early 1700's, this was not a populated area anymore and not disturbed. The area was referred as "an old, abandoned village". This early site in this region was carbon dated in 980 A.D. by the Monongahela Woodland Culture.

http://www.somersetcntypachamber.org/galleries/history/history-1.HTM

The Europeans was the first people in this area to hunt and trap. There were two men named Isacc Cox and Harmond Husband completely against the British government system. In 1869, they formed a group called the Regulators to fight against unfair taxes and fees. However, despite outnumbering the British soldiers; the British had better weapons and more ammunition. For these reasons, Husband and his fighting crew had to retreat.

http://www.somersetcntypachamber.org/galleries/history/history-1.HTM

In 1783, the town of Hannastown was destroyed. As soon as Husband heard of this, he wanted to move his precious family to Fort Cumberland for more of security blanket from Indian attacks. In 1784, Husband, Peter Ankeny and Ulrich Bruner made out plans for the town of Millfordtown. This town by people, who knew Bruner, called it "the town that Bruner laid out or Brunerstown.

http://www.somersetcntypachamber.org/galleries/history/history-1.HTM

During the Whiskey Rebellion era, (1790's) whiskey and grain was the value of business in this area. At first, there was no tax on whiskey for tavern owners to buy it or even sell it. Later on, the Congress would pass a bill because American government needed the money, so this was an idea to gain more of a profit towards building and developing the local community areas. For this reason, the people in Western Pennsylvania would rebel against the tax. This gave President Washington no choice in the early 1790's but to enforce the tax. It was witnessed that despite the 13,000 soldiers to uphold the new past tax law that Husband and General Robert

Philson of Berlin, Pennsylvania would represent their protest to building a liberty pole. They and others were arrested and tried but never convicted in a Philadelphia courtroom for their protests of this controversial tax. http://www.somersetcntypachamber.org/galleries/history/history-1.HTM

In 1795, the County of Somerset was formed from the town of Bedford. The community and area of Somerset County elected its first official, which was Alexander Addison. The past urban planning and development of Somerset County consisted of county jail of logs and soon to be courthouse. During the different eras of the three courthouses, the first courthouse lasted from 1801-1852 and was built of stone. The second courthouse consisted of brick, cupola, and two stories tall from 1853-1904. The final courthouse of which is standing today is much larger of the other two buildings. As the population and census increased, so did the need for a much larger building in 1907 as it is today. http://www.somersetcntypachamber.org/galleries/history/history-1. HTM

In 1804, Somerset became the first to be named a Borough. There would be three devastated fires that would happen to these citizens beloved town. The first one was in 1833 in which the first started from Edgewood Avenue and Diamond. The total damage of this past urban development was 80,000 dollars including: six stables, nine businesses, and ten ships total. Nearly forty years later in 1872, the second fire caused this small community was ninety buildings and 300,000 dollars' worth of damage. The final devastating fire was in 1876 in which it started at the stables of Somerset Foundry and moved eastward destroying homes, hotels and stores. http://www.somersetcntypachamber.org/galleries/history/history-1. HTM

Over the next forty years, the inventions and responsibilities would be even greater through electricity, light, water, and sewage. These technologies made the urban planning and development much easier because people in their communities had pipes running through their houses and homes instead of getting it through wells and rivers nearby.

Some houses had their own lighting through light bulbs. In 1879, William Gilbert was responsible for lighting lamps for a dollar a day, but not for no more for seventeen days out of each month. However, for any certain reason if there was an extra day or more, he was needed then he would get paid the extra dollar per day. This was only available five days a week. There would not be any twenty-four hours and seven days a week until 1914. In the early 1890's, several companies were developed in the Somerset County area to make the Somerset area more business-like and attract new people to their building town. These companies were the Somerset Phone Company, Somerset Water Works Company, Somerset Phone Company and volunteer fire department.
http://www.somersetcntypachamber.org/galleries/history/history1.HTM

The excitement of past citizens and planners of Somerset County from the village of Somerset of the early 1800's to the town size population development 1900's see a great growth and economic development through the great ideas and strides from our founding fathers. From our founding fathers to today as Somerset County residents, we must build the best community and urban plan possible to make the small area of Somerset better.
http://www.somersetcntypachamber.org/galleries/history/history-1.HTM

## Local Areas and Attractions of Somerset County

Kooser State Park Family Cabin District was built for the purpose of future camping development. This area was very significant for several purpose of the camp development which are: conservation, social history, architecture, landscape, entertainment, recreation, and politics. This state park is on the right side or eastern side of Mount Davis. This is also the location of where thousands and thousands of acres was destroyed by the May 31st and June 2nd Salisbury Tornadoes. This is about 8 miles away from Salisbury and 10 miles away from Rockwood. The period of significance was 1925-1949. This was added in 1987.

http://www.nationalregisterofhistoricplaces.com/PA/Somerset/state.
html

Mount Davis is the highest point in Pennsylvania located in Southwestern Somerset County at 3,213 feet in elevation. The reasons why so many people are attracted to this area of Somerset County are hiking, walking, running, picnic out, see deer and bear once in a while. This location also has a 100-foot tower to view two different states: West Virginia, and Maryland elevations range from 2500 to 3100 feet.

http://www.nationalregisterofhistoricplaces.com/PA/Somerset/state.
html

High Point Lake is a body of water about 15 minutes away fromMount Davis, Koosier State Park and Confluence. This area of attraction is from locals to fish and swim. This body of water flowsinto the Youghigeny River. High Point Lake Walleyed fish, Bass, Pike,and Catfish.

http://www.nationalregisterofhistoricplaces.com/PA/Somerset/state.
html

The Youghigeny River is a big-time river for fishing and the time for swimming especially in June through September. The YoughegenyRiver flows into the Monogehela River in the Pittsburgh area. The river has been above flood stages in the Confluence area in Januaryof 1996 at 29.0 feet which is about 2 feet above sea level. This caused schools and roads to be closed for several days.

http://www.nationalregisterofhistoricplaces.com/PA/Somerset/state.
html

The Laurel Hill State Park is located about 10 minutes away from Seven Springs Mountain Resort. The Laurel Hill State Park was built for out of staters to camp, fish and swim and enjoy the summertimein the beautiful area of Somerset County. The time period of whichthis place was significance was 1925-1949. This was an additionin 1987 to the National Register of Historical Places.

http://www.nationalregisterofhistoricplaces.com/PA/Somerset/state.
html

The Petersburg Tollhouse was added to the County's National Register of Historical Places in 1979. This area of importance is located off of U.S. 40 in Addision about 8-10 miles away from Confluence. The main importance of this location was transportation and road related situations. This is a museum in which the period of significance is from 1825-1849.
http://www.nationalregisterofhistoricplaces.com/PA/Somerset/state.html

The Somerset County Courthouse was added to the National Register of Historical Places in 1980. The courthouse system in this community has been around for 200 years. The main importance is for local government and law purposes. This is where court decisions have been decided for years. The period of time of significance is 1900-1924.
http://www.nationalregisterofhistoricplaces.com/PA/Somerset/state.html

All the related bridges of the Somerset County area from 1800-1949 were significant for one reason from the stagecoach era to the automobile era was transportation or to get a crossed one place to another. These places are: Barronvale Bridge, Beechdale Bridge, Jenner Township, Glessner Bridge, King's Bridge, Lower Humbert Bridge, New Baltimore Bridge, Shaffer's Bridge, Trotstletown Bridge, and Walter Mill's Bridge. These areas of Somerset County which they are located in Rockwood, Confluence, Somerset, Boswell, Stoystown, and Windber. These bridges of the Somerset County area and community were added to the National Register of Historical places in 1980.
http://www.nationalregisterofhistoricplaces.com/PA/Somerset/state.html

The following historical districts from 1991-2002 are: Windber, uptown Somerset twice, Stoystown, and Boswell. All of these districts were added through the different years above from the National Register officials of the local Somerset County area These different historical areas of Somerset County have period of significance from 1800-1949. The areas

of significances are architecture, community planning and development, social history, industry, and historical- non aboriginal.
http://www.nationalregisterofhistoricplaces.com/PA/Somerset/state.html

On September 11th, 2001, we will never forget what happened in Shanksville, Pennsylvania. The Flight 93 crew and passengers will always be remembered for the day they risked their own lives to stop theTerrorists from taking over the plane. This is why there is a Flight 93Memorial that will be forever lived as forty ordinary people changed theera for all time to come. These heroes prayed for strength, relief, faith and common courtesy for them uniting as one to stop at devastatingterrorist attack. These people deserve all are gratitude for such bravery and courage! http://www.flt93memorialchapel.org/

## New Business added

The confluence House Bed & Breakfast and Catering Services, LLC A Victorian style home, built in the early 1900's and located in the heart of Confluence. The Confluence House offers four guest bedrooms on the second floor and a spacious three-room suite on the top floor.

Rooms have queen beds, three private baths, air conditioning and most importantly, comfort. Relax on the front porch swing. Safely store your bicycles and gear in our locked garage. http://theconfluencehouse. com

The Garrett Bed and Breakfast is a place for tourists to stay and enjoy local activities in Somerset County. This Victorian Queen Anneis one of the oldest homes located in Garrett, Pennsylvania. It was builtin 1903 and is owned and operated by the seventh generation of thefamily Wanda Broadwater. It has spacious and luxurious rooms with acrowning touch turret necessary for a queen. Start your mornings witha delicious country homemade breakfast or a breakfast to go. We wantyour stay to be an enjoyable one and hope you'll experience unmatched comfort and convenience. http://www.garretthousebb.webs.com/

The Garrett House is the ideal location for your Somerset County and surrounding area plans. It is situated within a few blocks and easy access to the Bike Trail.

It is centrally located for the followingrecreational areas:

- The Great Allegheny Passage
- Windmill Farm
- Seven Springs, Hidden Valley and The Wisp Resorts
- Nemacolin Woodland
- White Water Rafting (Ohiopyle, Savage/Yough Rivers)
- Piney Run Golf Course
- Flight 93 Memorial / 9 Miners - Falling Water
- Kentucky Knob
- Yough and Cheat Rivers
- French and Indian War Sites
- Pennsylvania Maple and Autumn Glory Festivals
- Rails to Trails
- Hunting, Fishing, Camping, Hot Air Ballooning
- Somerset and Garrett County Fairs
- Mountain Playhouse
- Frostburg State University
- Amish Country ttp://www.garretthousebb.webs.com/

## Urban Development of Somerset County of Transportation and Activities

The Somerset County residents would like to see more hiking trailsand biking trails just like the specialized areas of Forbes State Forestand Laurel Highland hiking trails. There is a bike route that has notbeen developed, but this route is supposed to run from Pittsburgh toWashington D.C. The part of Somerset County has been completedby August 2001 and its 29 half miles long from Meyersdale toConfluence. The rest of the project from Confluence to McKeesportwas 71 miles long and was

finished a couple of years later. http://www.somersetcntypachamber.
org/scripts/chamber/site/AdventureSports.cfm

There are trips at a value of 200 bucks for interested Somerset
County people. This route now completed is total at 300 miles. This is
an eight-day trip and will bring more entertainment and more bikes
through the Somerset county area. The estimated total cost for this
adventurous trip would be 950 dollars with 20 people together. This
trip will prove of how effective this trail will be for urban business as
well. Will people actually want to move to an area like Somerset County
because of just an Allegheny Highland Trail, if you're a hiker, exerciser
then this is the place for you! Somerset County will always be a quiet
area with farming, cows, runners, walkers, hikers, bikers and of course
snowy winters.
http://www.atatril.org/yoktrek/2004trek.htm

There are other sports in Somerset County people enjoy, such as
whitewater rafting, hunting and fishing. The deer hunting in late
November through middle of December is big for county residents
because they are always looking for snow to make tracking deer easier.
People can enjoy whitewater rafting at Ohio Pyle. The hunters are glad
for the three state game lands of Gallitzin, Forbes State Forest, and Laurel
Hill State Park. These areas hunters can thrive on during the different
seasons of the year with variety of animals depending on the season.
http://www.nationalregisterofhistoricplaces.com/PA/Somerset/state.
html

There are also areas for fishing for local Somerset County residents.
These areas for citizens are Cranberry Glade Lake, High Point Lake,

Lake Somerset, Laurel Hill Lake, and Quemahoning Reservoir. The
location of Cranberry Glade Lake is about 8 miles South of Confluence
Route 3003. High Point Lake is 342 acres long and wide. Lake Somerset
is a half a mile away off of Route 219 in Somerset. The specific area and
location of Laurel Hill Lake is Laurel Hill State Park right off of Route
31 near Trent. The Youghiogheny River is located along Somerset and

Fayette County line in the Confluence area. This river is 2,800 acreslong and wide.
http://www.nationalregisterofhistoricplaces.com/PA/Somerset/state.html

## Enviromapper analysis of Somerset County

This map I printed out shows the different wastes and pollutants that danger the environment of Somerset County from the United States Environmental Protection Agency. There are several wastes and pollutants: water dischargers, superfund, hazardous waste, toxic releases, emissions and BRS. These waste and pollutants affect the following areas: Somerset, Friedens, Berlin, Meyersdale, and Rockwood. The most affected area is Somerset because of harmful toxic wastes and BRS from the most populated community in the county itself with the most business too. So, cars will cause smoke and so will well going businesses like food industries, factories, manufacturer companies. The coal mine areas of Meyersdale, Berlin and Boswell have trouble with hazardous waste and releases through cars, buildings and polluted rivers like the Casselman and Youghiogheny River.
http://maps.epa.gov/scripts/.
esrimap?name=enviroMapperN&Cmd=NavPan&CmdOld=ZO

## County Elected Officials of Somerset County Ideas

The different elected county officials of today are: James Marker-Chairman and Commissioner, Brad Cober- Commissioner, Pamela Tokar-Ickes Commissioner, Jerry SpanglerDistrict Attorney's Office, Wallace Miller-County Coroner, Carl Brown- County Sheriff, Donna Matsko Schmitt -County Treasurer, Shelley Glessener- County Auditor, Linda Jo BerkeyCounty Register of Wills, Patricia Brant- County Recorder of Deeds, and Mary Dinning- Clerk of Courts. These county elected officials have hopeful plans for Somerset County, such as better urban planning by building more businesses, and attractions. Projects from these elected officials are to clear polluted water from theCasselman

River of Meyersdale to Youghiogheny River of Confluence for better fishing and swimming conditions and to drink as well. Therehas been a recent electrical cleaner project in the Garrett, Somerset andMeyersdale area for the need for windmills in 2000. There are seven windmills in Garrett, ten in Meyersdale and ten more in Somerset fora more non pollutant protective environment.
http://www.naco.org/Template.cfm?Section=FindaCounty&Template=/cffiles/counties

## Somerset County of Planning Facts Population Percentages

The population of Somerset County was 79,553 people while thewhole state of Pennsylvania 12,287,150 people. Population percentchange was -0.6% while there was no change at all in PA. The population in 2001 in the county of Somerset was 80,023 people whilePA had 12,281,054 people. The population percentage change from 1990-2000 was 2.3 percent increase while in PA 3.4 percent increase. Somerset County is at a 5.2% in comparison to PA at 5.9%. Somerset County is at 22.3% in comparison to PA at 23.8%. The elderly of 65 years or older in Somerset County population percent in 2000 is 18.0% to PA's 15.6%. The percentage population of females in SomersetCounty in 2000 is 50.1% to PA's 51.7%. The white people population percent of Somerset County in 2000 is at 97.4% to PA's 85.4%. Black or African Americans population percent in Somerset County in theyear 2000 is 1.6% to PA's 10.0%. This data is supported by chart A.
http://quickfacts.census.gov/qfd/states/42/42111.html

## Education/Working Travel

People living in the same house in 1995 and 2000 population percentage of ages five and above is 70.6% in Somerset County and PA's at 63.5%. The foreign-born person in the year 2000 for population percentage in Somerset County is 0.7% in comparison with Pa's at

4.1%. The population percentage of High school graduates from 25 years and older in 2000 is 77.5% for Somerset County and 81.9 forPA. The Bachelor degree population percentage in 2000 in SomersetCounty is 10.8% and 22.4% in PA. The mean travel time to workin Somerset County is 22.5 minutes to the statewide average of 25.2minutes. This data is supported by chart B.

http://quickfacts.census.gov/qfd/states/42/42111.html

## Housing/Income

The housing units in 2000 in Somerset County are 37,163 to PA's 5,249,750. The homeownership rate for 2000 in Somerset County is 78.1% to PA's 71.3%. Somerset County is 11.9% to PA's 21.2%. The owner-occupied housing units for the median value in 2000 in Somerset County is $70,200 to $97,000 in PA. Somerset County is 31,222 to PA's 4,777,000. The person per household in 2000 for Somerset County is 2.45 to PA's 2.48. The household income for median purposes in 1999 for Somerset County is 30,911 and $40,106 for PA. The Per Capita money income in 1999 for Somerset County is $15,178 and $20,880for PA. The data is shown by charts C-F

http://quickfacts.census.gov/qfd/states/42/42111.html

## Employment/Sales

The Private nonfarm establishments in 1999 for Somerset County are 21,173 and 4,986,591 for PA. The percent change of nonfarm employment from 1990-1999 for Somerset County is 8.9% and 8.4%for PA. The non-employer establishments in 1999 for Somerset Countyis 4,309 and 614,594 for PA. In 1997, the manufacturers' shipments in Somerset County is 644,063 to Pa's 172,193, 216.The retail sales in 1997 for Somerset County is 543,075 to 109, 948, 462 for PA. The full-time equivalent and local government employment is 2,015 for Somerset County to Pa's 365,550. This data is supported by Chart G-I.

http://quickfacts.census.gov/qfd/states/42/42111.html

## Location Facts of Somerset County to Pennsylvania

The land area in 2000 in square miles in Somerset County is 1,075 to PA's 44,817. The persons that owned per square mile is 74.5 in Somerset County to 274.0 in PA. This data is supported by chart J-L below. http://quickfacts.census.gov/qfd/states/42/42111.html

## Conclusion

Somerset County in comparison with the state of Pennsylvania the population statistics have dropped slightly since the 1990's. The problem to this is getting solved with good Somerset County planner and citizen ideas by cleaning up the environment and attracting businesses to the beautiful quiet country area through great local government ideas aswell.

# CHAPTER 3

## Oklahoma City NBA Expansion Stadium Project

### Introduction

In expanding the National Basketball Association to Oklahoma City there are major factors that have to be taken into account. These factors include getting a background on professional sports expansion in order to get a clear view of how successful a team will be in the expanded area. Other factors are positioning the facility to house them so that it can be a recreational and cultural incentive to that area. The expansion site within a walking distance to other attractions would prove to be beneficial because it could possibly be a magnet for spectators within the Oklahoma City area. Also, drawing economically stable businesses to the area as well. This paper will give a literature review of various past expansion ventures that occurred throughout the country to confirm the potential site for the sporting facility and give a brief explanation of why the site was selected

# Literature Review of Sports Stadiums

Our literature review consisted of eight articles. We focused on past expansion sites, their success and failures, research studies on profitability of new stadiums and the "honeymoon period". It is through this literature review that we have substantiated our decision for placing a NBA stadium slightly north of downtown Oklahoma City. Below we have listed the articles we reviewed along with an article summary and opinion.

## An Empirical Review of the Stadium Novelty Effect

Howard, Dennis & Crompton, John (2003). Sports Marketing Quarterly. Volume 12, Number 2:111-117, 2003

## Summary

This article is to be an empirical review of two questions. The first question to ask is. Is there proof that a "novelty effect" happens when new stadiums are opened? The second question is. Who investigates if the franchises have better attendance with the new facility than without? Through research, they have discovered that 45% of all major league sports have constructed a new facility since 1995. Of these teams, the average attendance increase was 22.2%. However, they did note a decrease in each year following the opening season. This evidence supports the first question that there is a honeymoon period. Now to the important question most businesspeople want to know. Is the team better off with the new stadium? The answer is yes. Evidence showed that even though there were drastic decreases in attendance each year after the initial season. 9 out of 10 teams for which comparisons could be made showed appreciable gains in attendance over totals reported in the years preceding their moves to new facilities.

# Opinion

This article was good for our research because it proved that a new facility has a positive effect on attracting viewers. Also, it has hard data to back up its findings. Another positive point is this article stated that NBA teams had thebest increase in attendance related to a new arena.

NFL Teams Profiting From New Venues, By: Morell, John, Amusement Business, 00032344, 05/21/2001, Vol. 113, Issue 20

# Summary

A case between the NFL and the Raiders shed some light on financial balance sheets that the league has kept private. These balance sheets were shocking to confirm what we all thought. Teams with newer stadiums out ranked the other teams in operating profits. It concluded that the increased revenue streams that new stadiums bring are extremely lucrative. The article sited the Cleveland browns as an example. The Browns were last in the league for performance, but first in profits. It was stated that in 1999 they had an operating profit of $36.5 million. They were also first income from parking and advertising. As a result, the Cleveland Browns brought in $22 million. The glamour of these increased profits must not be taken out of context. A new expansion team and gain from a new facility does come with a price. The franchise fee for the Cleveland Browns to the NFL was $476 million. So, you truly do need money to make money.

# Opinion

I agreed with the article that new stadiums do increase the revenues for the teams. I learned that there are a lot of expenses that come with a new team that I may not have thought of before. This article helps us in planning our expansion site because of the real-life examples with the Cleveland Browns.

# Are Public Policies Needed To Level The Playing Field Between Cities and Teams?

Rosentraub, Mark S. (1999) Journal of UrbanAffairs; Dec99, Vol. 21 Issue 4, p377, 19p

## Summary

The NBA sports market forces a lifestyle for stadiums in suburban life in national transportation and housing programs. This also affects the imperatives of global competition followedby many leaders to think about how they must have attractive ideas to attract teams to the capitals of the states. (Kantor and David 1988) They concluded by saying "The structure ofmarkets had created a highly dependent position for cities."

All Communities can refuse to meet certain needs. The cities in some cases have most certainly dropped the issuefor bidding wars and firms, when the costs become too high. (Hudnut 1993; Nunn & Schoedel, 1995). The modern era of practice has provided many financial opportunities, but the most popular is subsidies. These are supposedto have attracted different teams after the 1953 season of sports. Baltimore was anxious to bring a MLB team; making the following attractions available by funding a second deck on Municipal Stadium and benefits of a loan to save the St. Louis Browns from going bankrupt made this possible. In 1954, the St. Louis Browns franchise was desperate to get out of town because of so many losingseasons. They decided Baltimore was a profitable area because of the attraction (Morgan, 1997). The year of 1956, Los Angeles wanted a franchise, so the Brooklyn Dodgers were persuading by several attractions, which included land, and other incentives. These incentives in persuasion for selection of specific locations were the choice of the owners. These incentives were ranged from tax abatements and expenditures for infrastructure to the people to buy luxury suites and unsold tickets. The professional sports teams now play their respective sports in public funded ballparks, stadiums and arena. These teams do not need to be responsible for its facility's capital and operational needs (Noll Zimbalist, 1997).

The NBA selects certain locations and areas for a new expansion team by also deciding how the revenues and players will be equally distributed between different market sizes and values. The communities not selected or advised to hold a team by the NBA will have to put more effort to satisfy their community. The result will be no possibility for an expansion team.

The biggest one of the investments for a ballpark was in Denver by Federico Pena, the mayor who brought MLB to Denver. This was quite important to the mayor as he quoted "I think if you're going to compete in the global marketplace you've got to step up to the plate, so to speak, in many areas, and one is you have to have a major sports teams in your city" (Whitford, 1993, p. 30). In 1997, the state of Indiana declared its matter of public reason to build a new arena for the Pacers which the legislature supported a tax supported plan of 109 million dollars for the new arena. Another example is in the NFL, when Indianapolis financed the Colts through the idea to convert tax dollars to the project of renting cars to finance the team.

## Opinion

In my opinion, this idea to create attraction to big cities with the money and smaller communities is a big disadvantage. The bigger cities have much more attraction with much more spending money. Some communities or cities have a budget to follow by and some do not. So, some cities cannot step up to the plate of opportunity to bring in a major league team. This is why it is a disadvantage.

## Cities, Sports, and Economic Change: A Retrospective Assessment

Rosentraub, M.S. (2002) Journal of Urban Affairs; Dec2002, Vol. 24 Issue 5, p549, 15p

# Summary

The fact that sports, tourism and entertainment are for recreational inventions or to undertake leadership is not very surprising. The cities involved have been central places of commerce, culture and cutting-edge occurring projects. The focus on urban renewal was developed because of the idea that center cities were flooded with criminals. The previous thought was different from recent thoughts of designing pictures of the cities and to make urban centers more attractive, such as diversity, tourism, culture, and commerce. That was the old focus, but the modern focus is involving trial and error in response to everyday economic changes and conditions within policy leading advising that resulted in equality between business and entertainment strategy. The period of the 1970's through the 1990's saw nearly all central cities; big suburban and other communities target their goals on downtown economy efforts on the hospitality industry. This trend would lead to the building of sports facilities all over the United States for all professional sports as a goal for the past 30 years. The smaller cities that are behind the modern sports facilities built in the modern age look on at Baltimore, Cleveland, Dallas, Denver, Indianapolis, and Phoenix have now made their goals towards minor league teams. The cities that have professional sports facilities show they let this economic development carry the load for the city's financial spending. Then, they tried to redevelop the strategy by giving up some space and area for a stadium for minor league teams. But, despite this fact, there are independent case studies in numerous facts that teams and structures surrounding it is not related with any city's economic development. Working together on several issues for any city has been about building facilities for all professional sports teams (Rosentraub, 1999, 2000). In the idea, these sports facilities can bring back the historical background between business, recreation, tourism, and downtown areas (Newman 2002).

# Opinion

In my opinion, over the last 30 years these coming attractions to downtown areas, such as arenas, stadiums and ballparks will be the future of all sports and profit. The coming attractions may sometimes work out or may not work out. This is why the higher city officials hope or assume the money and profiting will come in.

## Tourism, Sports and the Centrality of Cities

Turner, R.S., Rosentraub, M.S. Journal of UrbanAffairs; Dec2002, Vol. 24 Issue 5, p487, 6p

## Summary

The focus of incorporating the downtown area in the 1970's and 1980's was to build an effort for a corporate organization. The purpose of public sector resources was to reverse the falling property values (Frieden & Sagalyn, 1990). The businesses focused its goal on its interest in bringing retail activity back to the downtown to get more attractions to the stadiums in downtown areas. Commercial real estate rose to the occasion in the early 1990's. However, the festival marketplaces failed to produce positive answers. The cities started to turn to new forms of financial opportunity by supplying more tourist attractions, such as stadiums, arenas and parks. The cities would also turn to sports for the main attraction. The first major recent sports park to bring major attraction to downtown areas was the stadium that Baltimore built for the Orioles at Camden Yards This stadium definitely brought a pastime tradition to bring people to the ballpark through tourism, culture and entertainment. However, hockey and basketball weren't far behind as downtown areas tried to bring as much consumption of money as possible to their area. This was not always successful. As a result, city officials thought for sure it would bring more population, money, and immigrants to these areas.

The city's hope was a positive central city economic activity. One example is when people didn't want a team in Seattle. However, the Seattle baseball team was still approvedwithout any real results because of the money not materializing like it should have. The theory of the businesspeople of St Petersburg, Florida was to build a venue without any sports team and assume a team would bid on their area. However, this was not the case either to enhance their financial profits. This bidding, however, would have been a bad move for St. Petersburg because many cities got badfinancial deals. The downtown sports corporations were enthused by purchasing the naming rights to ballparks and stadiums. These newer sports facilities were used to attract higher financial standardsand select a certain audience through their advertisements.

## Opinion

In my opinion, the downtown areas, such as St. Petersburg, Seattle and Baltimore shows experiences of success and failure of persuading teams into their respective towns. This shows that cities are never guaranteed to get sports teams to their area no matter what they do through economic matters.

## The Impact of Stadiums and Professional Sports on Metropolitan Area Development

Baade, Robert A. Growth and Change, spring1990, Vol 21 Issue 2, pl, 14p, 4

### Summary

The debate about proponents of subsidization; it's a matter of planning the responsibility. In laymen terms, the responsibility of having a stadium exceeds its economic budget. The economic effort comes from all kinds of sources. These economic producingsolutions are rent, concessions parking, advertising suite rental and other preferred seating rental. However, direct expenses come from income wages, related expenses, utilities, repairs, maintenance, insurance policies and debt. Benjamin Oker (1974).

In the metropolitan areas, the rent pays the sports team's attendance. Let's give you an example, for instance, the Chicago Whitesox have signed a lease for twenty years. In the lease, it states The Chicago Whitesox will pay their landlord, (Illinois Sports Facilities Authorityor known as ISFA) for every seat sold 2.50 each 1.2 to 2 million and 1.50 with 2 million excess. This is for the first ten years of this lease, but the second ten years of the contract is a bit more expense because there is more to be paid off. Every seat sold $4.00 per ticket goes to the ISFA in excess to 1.5 million to 2 million sold and 2 million or more for 1.50 each ticket to ISFA. If this not the case that none of the expectations are reached then ISFA must purchase 300,000 tickets, if only the attendance is not met at 1.5 million. The Whitesox have a successful year in drawing at least 1.2 million people in the last 10 years of the lease. Then, the ISFA will pay the Whitesox 1 million per year. (State of Illinois 1988) In the Whitesox history have never drawn over 2 million respectively, but only in 1987 and 1988 have they ever drawn over 1.1 million per year.

## Opinion

In my opinion, when two higher businesses go out it to satisfy each other it's always a battle to win the war. I would never take the Chicago Whitesox to own or to finance a new stadium with because there has not been enough people coming over to see their games in a 50- year history and untilthis is proven then people will not come to the ballpark.

## The Employment Effect of Teams and Sports Facilities

Baade, Robert A., Sanderson, Allen R., Sports, Jobs and Taxes: the economic impact of sports teams and stadiums;Washington, D.C. Brookings Institution Press 1997

# Summary

This article focuses on the negligible increase in spending and new jobs. The types of jobs sports subsidies generate the cost of creating jobs through these subsidies. The spots facilities do bring in new jobs, while hurting the businesses that have already been in the area. The article also mentions that money earned by coaches, players etc. goes mainly into the national market, not local. The money earned may not necessarily benefit that area directly. Also, sports facilities that are built in areas where there is not a saturated sports market can prove to be economically beneficial as well. Jobs created by these new facilities are considered "trade" and "service" employment. These make up 98% of jobs creates by these sports facilities. Since these jobs are created by seasonal sports; they are part-time, which means this type of employment does not prove to be as beneficial as one might think. In addition to having these jobs created; they are often supported by having taxpayers sometimes payhundreds of thousands of dollars in order to support these positions.

# Opinion

As a taxpayer, I am appalled that my money goes toward something I have absolutely no interest in. There are bigger issues that need to be approached such as helping the sick and homeless. These facilities also run a high risk of hurting businesses that have already been in the area for some time. Take for instance, small family-owned businesses in the area; they may not surviveafter such changes are made. The "Powers that Be" would not really take this into consideration because it's not their mother'sbakery or their uncle's convenience store that will be suffering.

## Stadiums and Urban Space

Rosentraub, Mark S., Sports, Jobs and Taxes: the economic impact of sports teams and stadiums; Washington, D.C. Brookings Institution Press 1997

# Summary

Sporting facilities surrounded by acres of parking lots have different set of interaction than a facility within walking distance of restaurants, Office complexes, and other recreational facilities. This article states that recently people are more likely to migrate towards the suburbs. It goes on to say that when people shop, they have totally different feelings that are aroused than that from being at a sporting event. The two actions require separate types of energies to be evoked. Of the two cities studied, the results prove that population in those central business districts declined as well as job opportunities when sporting facilities were brought into the area. One of the cities managed to slow the suburbanization process by having a sporting facility that hosted many events of amateur teams that came from outside areas. When it comes to building sporting facilities to slow this decentralization process down those in charge of the project should proceed with caution because disappointed in this area occurs more often than not.

# Opinion

I think people try to come up with quick fixes to issues that affect their cities instead of looking at deeper issues that may in turn prove to be beneficial. Maybe that area could use a new shopping mall or lower taxes. There could be several reasons why those who live in central cities choose to relocate to suburbanized areas. Sporting facilities may seem to work for a short period of time, but eventually things will be the same or maybe worse. Building these facilities in troubled cities can be compared to a bandage. Bandages do not help wounds to heal; they only cover them up.

In conclusion, this literature review did help us decide where to place our stadium. We gained knowledge about the benefits of locating near restaurants and other attractions. Our group learned the importance of planning the financial cost of constructing. Also, the future economic impact of the stadium is with all possible parties to be involved. Through this literature review, we studied other cities successes and failures. We will be taking from their experiences to help make our project the most successful.

## Strengths of this area for expansion

Oklahoma City has many strengths. Their first strength is that they're 45th in the TV viewing market and have a population of 3,258,100. Secondly, Oklahoma City was ranked 2nd lowest for cost of doing business in the nation. Also, Oklahoma University is nearby and has developed a region of loyal sports fans. Finally, the city itself has many other tourist/leisure attractions. Here is a list of some of the local attractions: Remington Park Race Track, National Sports Hall of Fame, Lincoln Park, Forest Park, Edwards Park, Kirkpatrick Center, State Capital, Oklahoma Historical Society, Oklahoma City University, Oklahoma Art Center, and National Cowboy Hall of Fame Western Heritage Center.

We've decided the stadium will be built along two heavily traveled interstates I-35 and I44. The reasoning for this location is its proximity to local attractions and the availability of land. Remington Park Racetrack and The National Cowboy Hall of Fame Western Heritage Center are two of the closest attractions.

## Set up for new stadium

We began to make our base map with the data given to us. This included shape files such as Oklahoma City itself and a landmark polygon theme. These attractions include larger areas such as shopping centers, airports, and lakes. A landmark point theme shows landmarks such as a high school and a cemetery. Finally, the road shape file makes up of all the roads in Oklahoma City.

First, we changed the color of each theme in order to make it easier to distinguish between them. Second, we used the Identify Tool to identify the interstates. Third, we made them easy to locate with the addition of interstate symbols to the map. We also added graphics to the map indicating the hospital, the airport, and the Air Force base.

The first shape file we created on our map highlights the three interstates that run through the downtown area of the city includes I-35, I-44, and I-235. The next shape file we created indicates a half-mile buffer around the three interstates. This shape file is important because it aids us in placing the stadium approximately a half-mile from the interstate and insures us that the exit ramp will be approximately a half-mile in length.

The next step we took in the making of our map involved geocoding addresses of some of the most popular attractions Oklahoma City has to offer. By using the Measure Distance tool, we can affirm that the geocoded attractions range from about one to four miles in distance from the stadium.

The last two shape files that were added to the map indicate the stadium itself and the exit ramp leading from Interstate-44 to the stadium. Using the draw tool to locate a rectangle on the outer edge of the half-mile interstate buffer created the stadium. The rectangle was drawn carefully by first changing the distance units to feet under the View Properties menu in order to ensure that the stadium was drawn in a proper stadium size. Our stadium turns out to be approximately 821,000 square feet in size.

There are five maps included in the Attached Maps section of this paper. Each one portrays the steps taken in selecting and verifying the site for the new stadium.

# Conclusion

We concluded that this was the best possible site for our stadium in Oklahoma City because of the sporting attractions that include the National Sports Hall of Fame, Remington Park Racetrack, and the National Cowboy Hall of Fame, etc. Our facility would also be within walking distance to shopping venues, Parks, and other interesting attractions. These along with other components should be enough to attract new businesses and create new jobs as well. Although, there is no definite way to ensure a team's success with a new sporting attraction in this area, however, the odds are in our favor.

# CHAPTER 4

## Allegheny and Washington County Planning Studies

### I.) Problem defined: hypotheses, assumptions and theories

The problems with the region of western Pennsylvania are in the Washington and Allegheny counties that the results are lack of jobs, lack of income, population decreasing and a real sense of financial security. The reason for all of these problems is because the government puts more time into other things such as: cutting salaries for people, who have worked for a long time, laid off long time workers, and do not give the workers of Pennsylvania enough benefits. There are several reasons why the part of western Pennsylvania in general is struggling with the economic development.

The problems include the steel mills are gone from the early 1900's from which the brilliant Andrew Carnegie built in the early 20th century to boost the economy. As a result, thereafter workers would be out of jobs by the 1970's and 1980's from Donora to Pittsburgh. In this area, thousands of jobs would be lost because of no money being put toward the steel mills and bankruptcy would follow. There will have to be a need for more of every job just like there is in professional and clinical jobs in the near future.

# CHAPTER 4

## II.) Overview of Allegheny and Washington counties Whiskey Rebellion

The late 1700's saw a revolt against an excise tax on whiskey in 1791 that angered many American citizens. This was in the areas of Western Pennsylvania including: Washington and Allegheny counties. The results of this tax were to no satisfaction of the farmers as there would be no real business for selling or any importance of cash crop. The settlers would file disputes against the Federal Government for this reason.
http://www. earlyamerica.com/earlyamerica/milestones/whiskey/

The people in the Washington and Allegheny County regions were not accepting this tax well at all. There would be riots everywhere until the tax was lifted or lessened. The insurrection really opened itself to violence when tax collectors were attacked all the time. In July of 1794, several hundred men rebelled against an inspector by torching his home, barn and several buildings surrounding his home.
http://www.earlyamerica.com/earlyamerica/milestones/whiskey/

In Pittsburgh at the time, there was outrage there as well. So, on August 7th 1794, the President at the time, George Washington, had no choice, but to enforce the military under the 1792 Militia Law by protecting the union to make sure everything would be okay. The president's order was to set up at least 13,000 troops. This action resulted in the first official defense against rebellions in United States history. There were several arrests and they got out of jail after Washington pardoned them in Philadelphia.

http:// www.earlyamerica.com/earlyamerica/milestones/whiskey/

# National Road

George Washington and General Braddock originally founded the National Road in the mid 1750's. This road was used for military purpose. However, Thomas Jefferson thought of the idea to open the road further to extend travel to greater distances after buying the Louisiana Purchase for economic growth and development. However, this road would not be completed to Wheeling until 1818. This road would extend as far as Vandlia, Indiana in the 1830's, but with no funds the construction was stopped. The NationalRoad opened the Ohio River Valley for settlement and good economic development.

http://www.nps.gov/fone/natlroad.htm

The first years of the road being completed attracted frequent travelers to the west of the Allegheny Mountain. In this region, there was rich and fertile land to be settled upon by in the Ohio River Valley Region. This road's growth was also responsible for the increase in population. There were several cities along the National Road that was affected, which was Cumberland, Uniontown, Brownsville, Washington, and Wheeling. This road had economic growth by developing taverns, blacksmith shops and livery stables for travelers that went through small towns and villages. The main reason for this was so travelers and tourists had somewhere to go to make thembusiness or to stay the night.

http://www.nps.gov/fone/natlroad.htm

The taverns were by far the best business for the National Road because it was referred as the modern "truck stop". There were two kinds of these taverns, the expensive tavern was known as Stagecoach Tavern and the other tavern everyone could afford was the Wagon Stand. This tavern offered three different services, such as food, drink and lodging.

http://www.nps.gov/fone/natlroad.htm

The traffic would be outrageous during the day and early evening hours just like the Baltimore Beltway is today. The stagecoaches usually traveled for 60 to 70 miles per day. There was another type of transportation that only travelled 15 miles per day, which was the Conestoga Wagon. This wagon was referred as the 19th Century "tractor trailer". The Conestoga was developed to carry heavy weight west over the Allegheny Mountains. This design of this wagon looked like brightly paintedwith red running gears and also Prussian blue bodies and white canvas coverings.
http://www.nps.gov/fone/natlroad.htm

After 1850, the railroad industry started to take business away from the National Road and all was doomed from the start as all businesses especially taverns went out of business. The railroad was strongly not encouraged in the Pittsburgh area for the reason statedabove. However, the railroad would proceed into Pittsburgh by 1852. The B & O Railroad destination reached as far as Wheeling in the same year.
http://www.nps.gov/fone/natlroad.htm

In November1879, Harper's Magazine quoted "The national turnpike that led over the Alleghenies from the East to the West is a glory departed… Octogenarians who participated in the traffic will tell an inquirer that never before were there such landlords, such taverns, such dinners, such whiskey… or such an endless cavalcade of coaches and wagons." An unnamed poet quoted "We hear no more the clanging hoof and the stagecoach rattling by, for the steam king rules the traveled world, and the Old Pike is left to die."
http://www.nps.gov/fone/natlroad.htm

A new period of time began with the invention of the automobile in the early 20th century by Henry Ford. The National Road was revived after also being almost dead business wise because of the lackof travelers and businesses going bankrupt. However, the automobile would revive the National Road from a dirt road to a nice smooth paved road with business attractions replaced by the old taverns and other old business attractions with motels, hotels, restaurants and service stations to build the business what it would be today. However, some if not most of the traffic was diverted away because of two happenings the Federal Highway Act of 1921 and Federal Act of 1956 created a highway system of roads for Pennsylvaniaand other states as well.

http://www.nps.gov/fone/natlroad.htm

# Summary

The unemployment rating for Washington was slightly higher than Allegheny's from 5.9 to 5.7 in 2003. However, employment versus unemployment stats shows from 1996 to 1999 that employment was on the rise with unemployment down from 57.2 percent in 1996 to 50.1 percent in 1999. The table fromthe Pennsylvania economic development book shows a raiseof 12 to15 dollars per year from 1059.00, 1074.00, 1090.00 and finally 1,102.00. (2000- Pennsylvania Abstract Book)

According to the Pennsylvania economic development book, the jobs for whites outnumber blacks easily. In the region of Washingtoncounty and Allegheny County, the jobs for the white are higher for males from 190,167 to the females at 174,760. However, for the employment for the blacks, the female is out number from 19,070 to 14,365. The most popular position for whites in the Pittsburgh region is professionals. The most popular position for blacks in the Pittsburgh region is sales workers. (2000-Pennsylvania Abstract Book)

The population and income for 1999 between Washington and Allegheny is much higher because of the city of Pittsburgh and its 1 million populations but slow job decline and population projections show this to be true. These future population projections show from 2000- 2015 that an average of 30,000 to 45,000 people will leave the Pittsburgh and Allegheny by the year 2015. http://www.palmids.state. pa.us/INCOME.asp?geo,
http://www.palmids.state.pa.us/POPULAT.asp?geo

The population in 2000 was 1,265,184, but by 2015 will be 1,157001. The employment projection according to the U.S. Bureau of Labor Statistics in November 2001 will need morejobs for physician assistant services will increase 53 percent by 2010. Also, the job profession is one of the top 15 growingjobs people go to for a living. According to a National PA Demographics fact, there was a per capita distribution of 8.83 per100 K population ranks 32 out of 50 states. http://pittsburgh. bizjournals.com/pittsburgh/stories/2003/08/25/daily12.html

The average person would make about 7,000 dollars more near Pittsburgh than in Washington, PA. There are about 1 million people more in Allegheny than in Washington. Theseresults show the economy is dying because of the population projection drops slightly every five years. Despite, the late 1990's surge for income and wage improvement when GovernorRendell in the early 21$^{st}$ century, he took over, it was all downhill from there. (2000- Pennsylvania Abstract Book)

The average weekly earnings went slightly up each year from 1997 to 1999. The average weekly hours dropped slightly from 43 to 42.5 from 1997 to 1999. The average hourly earnings show a slight rise from 14.71 to 15.3 by 1999. Allegheny County has the advantage for money coming and dominates every economic type of job, such as services by 10 million dollars, manufacturing by 4 million, government enterprises by 2.5 million, and about 2,500 more dollarsin farming than Washington as well. (2000- Pennsylvania Abstract Book) For additional information, these charts below will provide alldata of employment from Washington County and Allegheny areas.

## Conclusion

In Conclusion, the economic development stats show slight rises in wages, income and whites working more than blacks in the late 1990's. However, since Rendell has taken over Washington and Allegheny counties have unemployment rates of 5.9 percent to 5.7 percent. The population projects show that the economic interest in this area and state of Pennsylvania will drop unless there will be more tourist attractions. Statistics will have to show in the near future in favor of every kind of job possible justlike in the professional fields and clinical fields, but we must have a better leader than Rendell or all hope will be lost.

# CHAPTER 5

## Running furniture Store and Expanding

### Introduction

In week six, this finance learning team assignment must reflect around analyze the effect of price setting on capital budgeting. There must be solid explanations of each of the methods, pitfalls, and benefits of capital rationing. Finally, this group must create an effective financial plan that explains everything about Guillermo's Furniture Store Scenario. With an effective financial plan in mind, the group members responsible will need to analyze of what the problems might be and give a solution to set price setting on capital budgeting.

Our recommendation for Guillermo Furniture's problems of foreign competition and increased labor cost is to align the organization with the high-tech option. This paper will provide a justification for this recommendation and provide a five-year pro forma cash flow budget for the organization. Guillermo Furniture has made the decision to invest in the high-tech automated equipment for mass production of furniture which will reduce the company's overall labor cost. Because the increase in population and jobs in Sonora have lead to a rise in the cost of labor, whereby, making it difficult for Guillermo to keep prices as competitive as before.

# Recommendation

With the current situation of rising labor costs and foreign competition, Guillermo must change its business strategy to survive in this market. One option for Guillermo is to maintain its current course of action. The second option would be to utilize the Norway firm and the distribution channels. The final alternative is the high- tech option, which Team C feels as the best choice. The choice of the high-tech route is that it presents the most comprehensive response to growing labor costs and threats posed by competitors using this option. A third option preserves the integrity of the company by lowering labor costs and avoiding the influence that the Norwegian company would create. From this perspective, the high-tech method presents the best option to lead Guillermo into a successful future.

# Foreign Competition

The option of forming an agent relationship with the Norwegian organization is a possible alternative that allows them to remain competitive. With this option Guillermo can shift its focus solely to distribution. However, the disadvantages, as shown in the scenario are that Guillermo would now have less control and more responsibility. Most of the custom work which originally established the organization would not be a viable alternative for the company. This merger could potentially have an impact on the patented process for furniture coating, especially since there will be new owners with the merger.

The patented process that Guillermo holds for coating the furniture creates a common flame-retardant, and ultimately stain resistant. There is market for the flame retardant, but not as much of a market for the finished coating (University Of Phoenix, 2009). These products can be marketed and sold together. Having multiple product lines will allow Guillermo to diversify its risk while capitalizing on the company's reputation.

The high-tech option would mean that several major purchases would have to be made initially. The budgeted figure in this forecast is a profit despite of increase in equipment price. This option would reduce human error, and allow Guillermo to run a 24/7 operation,which would present large savings in their future production costs.

## Labor Cost

The first option of Guillermo Furniture continuing without any changes is the least acceptable option. In Sonoma Guillermo Furniture Company is currently facing continually rising labor costs, smaller profit margins and lost market share due to foreign competition. Guillermo Furniture needs to take some corrective action in lieu of remaining unchanged.

## Justification

Team C will provide justification that the high-tech option is the best alternative for Guillermo. The first situation that Guillermo is faced with is their labor costs to manufacture the quality furniture with a slight premium. Guillermo has been fortunate in the past and experienced relatively low labor rates. However, with all of the industrialization occurring in Sonora and the new entry of people raised the cost of labor significantly.

The second situation that Guillermo has to come is the overseas competition entering the market. The foreign competition hurt Guillermo's business because of its high-tech approach, thus a lower labor cost which allowed the competition to offer the same products and with lower prices. This high-tech approach will be expensive in the short term. This will allow Guillermo the opportunity to reduce the labor needs as well as providing the opportunity to manufacture new product lines. By increasing productivity levels with the new high-tech approach

Guillermo will in the near future increase the company's profitability and be more competitive.

Guillermo is very hesitant to consolidate with other organizations so with this in mind he is forced to seriously consider the foreign competitions high-tech solutions. Guillermo will need to begin manufacturing new products that will permit Guillermo to be more competitive. There are significant changes occurring in the Sonora's economy as well as foreign competitions hightech advancements creating changes in the furniture manufacturing market.

The recommendation Team C has developed is that Guillermo needs to consider that the high-tech approach. Although this approach will incur significant expenses initially it would be safe to assume that there will be a higher level of return in the future. This initial capital investment of high-tech equipment is the best solution to make sure that Guillermo stays viable in a changing market.

## 5 Year Pro Forma Cash Flow Budget

Per our team's recommendation on urging Guillermo to go high-tech a five-year pro forma cash flow budget should be reviewed. The purpose of generating this pro forma cash flow is to forecast Guillermo's profitability levels in the future. In order for Guillermo to move ahead they will need to use current cash, credit, leasing or other financing options.

There are several advantages to utilizing a cash budget. This process will provide Guillermo with the best estimate on how operations should be planned for the next five years. Another benefit is drawing Guillermo's attention to its cash resources. In order to create a projected expense and revenue estimates we must take a look at Guillermo's income statement. The purpose of this budget is to be a financial control tool for Guillermo.

A cash flow budget reflects the evaluation of financing requirements, production plans, and marketing measures, but it will not measure the profitability levels. This pro forma statement will allow us to project future financial statements based on the future funding needs and performance. Thus, we will use the Guillermo's cash budget information so that we can estimate the revenue from the furniture sales. We will also be using the cash budget information in order to get a ballpark figure of what the high-tech expenses are going to be in the future as well. Another factor we need to consider is the depreciation of the high-tech equipment we will purchase and or lease. Technology changes quickly and we need to make sure that the depreciation is factored into our forecasts. We can already see that production can be increased by 50% from the current mid-grade level going towards the high-tech option.

The best option for Guillermo based on the income information is going to be to purchase the equipment. In the future the reduction in salaries, benefits, will outweigh the increase in the insurance and property taxes based on the data provided. Guillermo needs to stay competitive in order to meet and or beat foreign competition. By reducing labor costs and investing in high-tech equipment Guillermo looks to be more productive and viable in the future.

## Conclusion

In conclusion, after analyzing Guillermo Furniture Store's alternatives, Team C did make a recommendation to choose the high-tech route and make justifications based on the recommendation. A pro-forma cash flow budget has also been created for Guillermo's next five years to show cash inflow and outflow and it is also used for internal planning. Team C believed that the suggestion will help Guillermo to save in labor costs, to keep his business thriving within the competitive market, and to lead his store into a successful future.

# CHAPTER 6

## Running a Food Service West Coast Business

### Introduction

This proposal explains to upper management the recommendations for specific job descriptions for new positions for Kudler Fine Foods. The company has an effective training program for new and current employees to introduce and enhance skills. The proposal has to include feedback, evaluation, and compensation methods from previous weeks of research. Furthermore, the plan needs are an effective career development plan that address unique needs for a team appraisal system, team motivations and expectations, equality of each individual's performance and its effects, social loafing, individual responsibilities within the company, incentives, benefits, strategies for managing education, diversity, and a fair compensation plan. All these ideas have to be for a company to succeed.

### Job Analysis

Kudler Fine Foods is looking to hire a food sales manager, assistant food sales manager, baker, wine maker, and cheese and production worker. (Apollo Group, 2007) The manager and the assistant manager will have solid experience in food service sales or a related65 field. The manager salary range is $35,700 to $42,500 dependingon experience. The assistant manager salary range is $30,200 to 33,500 depending on experience. These positions will make $9.00 per hour with monthly evaluations. High school diploma is required. The candidates must possess good communication and leadership skills. These candidates will have business knowledge of food sales, product, equipment and money handling. Candidates will have at least five years experience in a food management team environment. The candidate for baker, wine and production positions have one year experience in food service. (Apollo Group,2007) Education in business administration is a plus for qualified candidates for manager and assistant manager positions. The reason for these five new positions are Kudler is adding another store in California and food production and sales experience for three shifts full-time and two full time managers to run operation expenses. The future of these positions is to build more stores, a great food service and customer service environment. Kudler Fine Foods has had a great reputation with there three stores let's make California are building ground for business! (Apollo Group, 2007)

## Training and Mentor Needs

The most effective training for new and current employees with Kudler Fine Foods is through the use of videos that demonstrate astep-by-step process through communication, sales, profits, companypolicies, procedures and satisfactory performances. The Kudler Fine Foods will be using on-line computer quizzes and testing scenarios to adequately evaluate the level of knowledge pertaining to areas of job situations, handling inadequate job performance results, and how to approach customers effectively. The objectives of the training and mentoring programs are to get the employees of Kuddler Fine Foods to understand how to sell effectively and becomesuccessful in striving for the highest customer service levels through knowledge of food taste, value, health and production standards.

## Delivery Methods

The Delivery methods are keys to the employee's success because as a teacher or trainer the group has to realize what facts are important to learn and is not. A trainer has to be motivated, dedicated and knows how to direct problems. A trainer's delivery method affects employee's results in training and afterwards because the trainer should know about expectations of the company, such as food servicesales techniques, profit margin hints, communication problems, and how to handle customers and other coworkers with disagreements. Trainers should use delivery methods, such as meetings, testing and evaluation of course, and work expected of every employee. These trainings will heavily depend on employee's success results.

## Training Content

The proper training content for Kudler Fine Foods is to improve performance of workers within the company and get new workers excelling above company's expectations. With the extensive training content companies like Kudler Fine Foods are offering, the probation period becomes critical in determining employee's work performance within the company. The probation period is 90 days. They expect employees to arrive on time to all trainings to be prepared for intensive face-to-face training. Another set of training are step-by-step videos on selling techniques and test evaluations to determine the extent of knowledge about the company policies and procedures with product pricing and usage. These trainings will provide how to handle money, different foods, such as cheese, bakery and other gourmet foods for proper knowledge.

# Feedback and Performance Development

Kudler's Fine Foods management feedback will be given for all new and current employees on job performances based upon their attitude, knowledge, skills, and customer surveys. The difference between individual and group appraisal is based on how effective a person will do working alone and each member of the group working to different expectations. Individual and groups are monitored in the same ways but from time-to-time groups members work should be equal because some people are plain lazy and will affect groups performance. The difficulty of evaluating team performance is how much each team member did and assesses how well the group worked together. This feedback will help determine how successful the candidates will be with Kudler Fine Foods from an individual to group project. The selected people for Kudler Fine Food's team will be appraisal system to excel in a critical company component and wants in the areas of food management and sales, in order to obtain promotions and salary increases. The company's feedback review is critical to all employees in letting them know their strengths and weaknesses. Kudler Fine Foods believes that honesty is the best policy with all employees and their performance levels. The evaluation process strengthens the relationship between management and the group in order to offer additional training as needed. Social loafing will not be tolerated! All employees are expected to work while on company time. An employee is unable to validate what their particular work assignment is. The employees are to speak with management for clarification.

For employees needing further development in communication, food service management sales and profit understanding, product understanding of company's expectations, and handling customer rejection. Kudler will pay for all further training through travel training programs. The employees and superior have concerns about a worker's skills. Then, Kudler Fine Foods is dedicated to providing all available training to help improve individual and company success. Additional training methods such as practicing with group members on product presentation techniques will also be readily available. For those who wish to work independently, the company offers demonstration and motivation tapes in one of several offices.

## Performance Standards

The performance standards for Kudler Fine Foods are to remain positive with respect to one's attitude and job environment. Performance standards are categorized by the customers' feedbacksurveys and the level of satisfaction received from their customer'sevaluation. Kudler will also monitor how effective an employee isin different performance situations through multitasking, phone communication, sales and profits through food services and employee's knowledge of each individual food product. There will be disciplinary action to employees disobey the rules and policy of Kudler Fine Foods. Employees are expected on time because the employee is late for no good reason. This will as a result be written up. No parking in customer spot areas or a write up will be necessary. No using vulgar language around customer or termination will be a good possibly. No stealing or giving out free food to customers or friends. Physical conflicts or fights will resultin suspension or immediate termination. As a result, three write ups and look for another job! Kudler Fine Foods is dedicated to hiring responsible employees and not irresponsible employees!

## Compensation Plan

This compensation plan will consist of salary bonuses up to 15 percent, more vacation time and promote outstanding employees who meet the company's expectations. Kudler Fine Foods would like to introduce direct deposit for easier convenience. There will be opportunities for employees further their education through company-sponsored scholarships and will have option of company-paid volunteer opportunities. The salary bonuses will be determined by the consistent level of commitment, employee contributes to the company's increase in customers and production through food service. Vacation time will be allocated to top-level employees, who have a good performance record, no write-ups, and acceptable attendance. These employees have to be with the company for at least six months to be eligible for a week (five business days) vacation. Kudler Fine Foods understands that family emergencies occur. The company offers paid leave up to five business days for all emergences as categorized under the employee handbook. Kudler Fine Foods is devoted to keeping all employees happy and healthy.

## Proposal of Pay System

The reasons the pay system will work is Kudler Fine Foods is dedicated to satisfying expectations of customers and employees as well. Therefore, we are dedicated to rewarding for their hard work and dedication to Kudler Fine Foods with satisfying and motivating pay structure. The company will evaluate all employees on a monthly basis instead of every six months. Vacation time will be based on performance, attendance, consistent demonstration of outstanding performance for the company. Employees are eligible for vacation after six months of continuous employment. Employees working for the company for three years will get an extra week vacation (five business days) for every six months of continuous performance with the company. Kudler Fine Foods understands their employee's work. Kudler wants to reward our employees with a competitive salary and extra vacation time. A final incentive is the addition of direct deposit. This will allow our employees to avoid long drives to their banks and any checking-cashing fees.

The strategies for managing career development are furthering education and reimbursement for volunteering are supplementary forms of appreciation to employees facing the everyday challenge of satisfying difficult customers. The education needs to have enhanced skills to boost an employee's career. All volunteers represent the company will be fully reimbursed. There is no limit of reimbursement because Kudler wants to make employees feel like they are appreciated for non-paid work just as much as paid work.

## Three Components

The three major components of this benefits package are more evaluations for all employees will offer the chance for wage increases sooner than the current six-month evaluations under the old policy. There will be healthcare benefits after 90-day probation period for full-time employees. The health care will cover work related accidents and taken out of employee's paycheck weekly. The cost will be roughly 10 dollars a month. The highest-rated performers will be recognized with pay raises, ranging up to 15 percent, and vacation time. Furthermore, performance evaluations by the manager will be based on a 100-point scale monthly. This will determine any earned pay raised rather than the current, and more elaborate rating scale of 600 points after the six-month evaluation. 15 percent raise will occur of scores over 540. 10 percent raise will occur of scores over 480. 5 percent raise will occur of scores over 420. Below 420 scoring is zero.

## Explanation of Compensation plan's Benefitsto Employees/ Kudler Fine Foods

Attention all employees and company representatives, the following new plan for compensation benefits has been proposed in order to offer a more comprehensive benefits package. Kudler Fine Foods would like to announce several changes that will be taking place. Direct deposit will be offered to eligible employees. Kudler Fine Foods offers educational scholarship opportunities and company-sponsored volunteer opportunities.

Additional incentives in the form of salary bonuses, vacation time and monthly performance evaluations will be enacted. The salary bonuses will go to employeesmeeting company requirements on overall performance and customer satisfaction, length of employment time and attendance. Monthly evaluations will determine employees in expectations with Kudler. These evaluations will be assessed collectively six months to determine employees' eligibility for a pay raise up to 15 percent range. Vacations will be available by company policy to employees with Kudler for six months. Healthcare is affordable for 10 dollars per month and covers all accidents at workplace. An employee with wife and children covers 4 people with no cost.

(Family Coverage) Kudler Fine Foods would like to announce paid personal leaves, evaluated on a case-by-case basis for up to five paid days for situations arising from a family emergency or sickness.

## Summary

This career development plan summary should improve employee motivation to not only sustain a lasting and growing relationship within the company and customer service.

The performance evaluations for these new five employees are fair to succeed for promotions. Kudler Fine Foods feels there is no better company to work to improve internal and external satisfaction. Direct deposit, education and volunteer opportunities are here! Kudler Fine Foods has improved monthly evaluations, initiated salary bonuses and vacation time as great motivators for current employees and future recruitment.

# CHAPTER 7

## Business Law Practices and Principles

### Introduction

The Objective of this paper is to describe the four different types of alternative dispute resolution. There are four types of alternative dispute resolution are to be discussed are arbitration, mediation, summary of jury trials and peer review. (Jennings, 2006) There will be descriptions of the process of ARD and resolutions to cut down costs for parties involved in disputes. (Jennings, 2006)

### ARD TypesArbitration

Arbitration is solving money disputes between baseball player and team. The player wants more than the team pays. These people go to court to resolve money dispute between an arbitrator. In contract disputes, the contract states to have issues resolved between the two parties listed above. (Jennings, 2006)

# Mediation

Mediation is described as parties coming to a resolution and less expensive. (Jennings, 2006) The mediator does not issue a decision. (Jennings, 2006) Mediation does not require disputing companies to have lawyers. (Jennings, 2006) The parties unless agreed upon has no binding in mediation process on an agreed bonding term by decision. (Jennings, 2006) For example, Amazon.com and EBay has settled their disputes through this process. (Jennings, 2006)

# Summary of Jury Trials

Summary of jury trials is an ARD process both parties show evidence for the judge and jurors. (Jennings, 2006) The resolutioncomes through the jury first to give an advisory verdict for both parties. (Jennings, 2006) Both parties disagree then a trial begins. (Jennings, 2006) Both parties get ideas from jurorsand guidelines for resolution to problem. (Jennings, 2006) This process of ARD saves money after expenses are spent and results late in the process of litigation. (Jennings, 2006)

# Peer Review

Peer review is an ARD process used between employers and employees to resolve problems, such as termination, demotion, and discipline. (Jennings, 2006) Companies use this process, such as Darden Industries are associated with Red Lobster and Olive Garden to reduce expenses and employee litigation. (Jennings, 2006)

# Summary

In this paper, four ARD processes are described and what the down sides and up sides about each are. Employer has a choice to what process to choose to resolve issues through less cost and stress.

# Company Overview

The purpose of this paper is to discuss about Gene One Scenario. (University of Phoenix, 2009) Gene One is a classic example of an organization that thrives on rapid gene technology innovation and has charted unparallel growth following its niche market strategy in a short period of eight years. The company exploited its main competitive advantage – its ability to innovate rapid launch of genetically manipulated and disease resistant agricultural products –under the dynamic leadership of Don Ruiz and his team comprising several other resourceful founder members and became a UD$ 400 million enterprises from a modest US$ two million in 1996. The company has been performing well because its inception as a privately owned enterprise; however, in response to rapid changes in environment and competitive dynamics in the industry and to sustain it growth the company requires notable investments in and restructuring of its functional areas like sales & marketing, Research and Development (R&D), Production, Human Resource, Operations along with changes in the leadership team. As a result, it is aggressively looking at an Initial Public Offering (IPO) to ward- off its financial constraints and to develop capabilities in relevant areas. This vision and new perspective of the company poses two challenges in front of the senior leadership which is devising a strategy to successfully roll out IPO within 36 months – it includes challenges such as facilitating changes in the organization to meet Sarbanes-Oxley Act (SOA) guidelines, boosting company image, maintaining good growth (40% growth targets) and continuous innovation and development of new products ahead of the IPO to boost investors sentiments - and devising an organizational strategy to prepare the organization for this change that looks currently unreceptive to such changes. Further, the matter became worse due to untimely death of company's Chief Executive Officer(CEO) shortly after the announcement of the IPO that not only added another challenge in front of the board and Ruiz Family of appointment of new CEO but also posed significant threat to the very idea of going public in current situations. (Kotter, J.P., 1996)

# Future Vision – Goals and Challenges

The company have set an aggressive target for the next 3 years and thus need to offset a number of challenges in attempt to realize those targets that ranges from developing capability to constantly innovate and introduce new products to investment in production and R&D facilities, branding, marketing, corporate culture changes, organization structure and control changes, change in constitution of board and successfully driving company reputation in the market to garner investor's interest. (Kotter, J.P., 1996)

On the other hand, the successful transition of company from a small-scale privately owned company to a public limited company would offer numerous advantages that cannot be neglected at this point in time considering the increasing focus of investors in biotechnology companies and leadership changes taking place at Food and Drug Administration (FDA). The public offering is expected to provide the company ample financial resources along with several other sustainable competitive advantages such as increased visibility and recognition, ability to explore potential global markets with its existing niche products, more access to market capital and investors, ability to attract competent work force and technology experts, ability to forge industry relationship and increased operational efficiency among others. (Kotter, J.P., 1996)

# Proposed Change Strategy for the Company

As outlined above, the company is facing three main challenges currently which are appointment of a competent CEO to take company's end vision forward, identification of concern areas and devising an effective strategy to prepare for the proposed IPO and determination of organization change process that motivates the organization to accept radical changes in structure and leadership warding-off prevailing insecurities related to jobs and future prospects, fear of failure, complacency among the employees, corporate culture issues such as threats to values and ideals, team conflicts, loss of talents, polarization of employees and communication issues. A suitable strategy is being proposed for all three changes under the following subheads, however, the main idea behind these recommended strategies is to guide change incrementally with collaborative practices instead of forcing it at one go. (Kotter, J.P., 1996)

## CEO Appointment and Leadership Strategy

The most challenging task before the executive board and Ruiz family is the appointment of a new CEO who can lead the successful transition of the company and can achieve the end vision objectives. The appointment of a new CEO from within the organization is recommend keeping the view firstly, appointing an outsider for the post may well make the situation worse, secondly the person who has been associated with the company from the past will have greater understanding of the current corporate culture, focusareas during change process, employees' concerns and greater communication with leadership team. All potential candidates should be judged using a transparent process as it may lead to further escalations in senior management team. The process should include the evaluation of potential candidates on parameters such as motivation level for change, style of leadership, possess clear roadmap and vision for the change strategy, ability to increase collaboration among his team and the organization though his cogent abilities, his/her organization image and acceptability as the leader and the competence level.

Also, the constant monitoring of the newly appointed CEO is to be ensured until his/her acceptanceas a leader in the organization. The re-building of the leadership team should be continued only after the appointment of the CEO, and he/she should be given reasonable freedom while building of the team. The new executive team is recommended to have a good mix of old and new talents. Also, professional with experience with an IPO and instrumental in leading change must be given preference during the selection of board members and other executives. The leadership team must adopt participative leadershipstyle during the entire change process. (Banham, H., 2005)

## IPO Rollout Strategy

Considering the fact that the proposed IPO has been much advertised by media, change of mind would be more detrimental as it will put a question mark on the leadership and organization's capabilities to go public besides making required financial support inaccessible to the company due to postponement of the IPO.

Therefore, a detailed roadmap needs to be prepared with key target allocation and resultant changes to be made with strict timelines attached to it and the same should be communicated within the organization. Changes should take place incrementallywith careful monitoring in such a way that it should not disturb the organization's current functioning and productivity. A more experienced Chief Financial Officer (CFO) should be appointed with sound knowledge in financial reporting and IPO process. Further, Auditing, compensation and nomination committees should be created to meet IPO requirement. (Kotter, J.P., 1996)

## Organization Structure Change Strategy

The future goal of the company cannot be realized without the co-operation of the people who has worked for the organization makingit a success in a short-span of 8 years, customers and suppliers. Therefore, a change strategy has to consider all dimensions of theorganization such as corporate governance (people, structure and control mechanism), resources (R&D, Marketing and Financial),customers and shareholders. As affecting any change in the corporate structure directly affects the corporate culture which in turns affects employees, customers and suppliers therefore before initiating any radical change increased communication among stakeholders becomes important. (Bauer T., Erdogan B., 2010)

The organizational change should start with the communication process that demonstrates the need of change, create convergence among employee, convey the role of individuals during the process, assures better future prospects, assess the degree of resistance to change and minimize the related concerns, fear and misconceptionsthrough discussions. Once the awareness is assured and new changevision is communicated to the satisfactory levels, structure changes should be initiated department-wise, and employees should be made accustomed to these new changes in organization culture. Employees can be simultaneously trained for new skills to improveperformance and guided about their activities in newly changed environment which would bring in them a sense of empowerment,ward-off insecurities related to lack of skills and create in them ability and motivation to respond to changes efficiently. In order to minimize team conflicts and to develop cohesiveness and peer learning, teams with good mix of old and new employees should be created. All department heads should work collaboratively in allocation of resources to build departmental capabilities to achieve growth targets. Employees responsible for handling teams should be trained on team building skills. Initially, employees should be given short-term targets in line with the main vision and achievers should be rewarded by implementing a transparent performance appraisal system which would significantly boost confidence of employees. (Bauer T., Erdogan B., 2010)

## Final Thoughts

Initiating change in an organization is not a one-step activity but is a process which comprises eight-stages described as establishing a sense of urgency, creating the guiding coalition, developing a vision and strategy, communicating the change vision, empowering employees for broad-based action, generating short-term wins, consolidating gains and producing more change and anchoring new approaches in the culture

(Kotter, J.P., 1996). Inability of the leadership to manage change at any of these stages will significantly results in the failure of the entire process. Leadership team serves as the guiding light of the change process and set the tone as how the change will be affected. At Gene One also, the newly appointed CEO has to make sure that everyone on the executive team is prepared for the transition, work in cohesion and implement a collaborative approachwith a strong positive belief about the future the transition would bring in for the company. Further, the leadership team should be accessible to employees to promptly address any originating questions or concerns.

The emphasis should also be on preparing employees for the change through training, frequent employee meetings and one-to-one feedback or communication. Also, the newvision of the Gene One can be advertised in form of a 'slogan' or 'phrase' at different places such as in departments, at bulletin boards or in the form of computer wallpapers and in the email signature to create more awareness making transition seamless. Employees should be informed and convinced well in advance on what changes to expect related to their future role and performance in the changed environment after the transition to create greater convergence and trust within the organization. (Kotter, J.P., 1996)

## CHAPTER 8

### Resolving Company Disputes

#### Introduction

The purpose of this paper is to describe a problem within an organization, such as Kudler Fine Foods in which it focuses management to resolve company's issues and get results! (Glaid, 2009) The rest of problem-solving model step by step is throughsuggesting ideas in the right frame approach to describing the company goals from beginning to end. (Glaid, 2009) The problem within Kudler Fine Foods is they need more help because there are so many responsibilities. (Kudler, 2003)

#### Kudler Fine Foods

Kudler Fine Foods is a great company expanding. (Kudler, 2003) However, there is a problem statement that needs to be answered. What can Kudler Fine Foods do with an organization that is growingbut has a small group of people doing a lot of responsibilities?

The result is simple hire the most qualified candidates as soon as possible to fill much needed positions in all stores to make companyrun easier for Kathy. (Glaid, 2007) However, the next step in the problem-solving model is doing it with the right approach because the owner KathyKudler makes all final decisions on how many to hire and who should be added. (Glaid, 2009) So, every decision is critical. The owner Kathy may be busy, so a meeting may need to be called to fill needed wholes and to discuss further business about adding additional people. (Glaid, 2007)

Kathy decides to add several positions to each of her stores to lower the workload for herself and others. (Glaid, 2007) This resolves any issues of notenough labor or too much person for one person. (Glaid, 2007)

According to Kudler Fine Foods, "Kudler Fine Foods is committedto providing customers with the finest selection of the very best foods and wines so that your culinary visions can come true." (Kudler, 2003) In my opinion, for a food service business to run properly, you need the proper staff to run one position not one personrunning three positions for this type of business to run smooth.

According to the Kudler Fine Foods site, the beginning visionis to have Kudler Fine Foods will be the premiere gourmet grocery store for those savvy shoppers who are searching for the best meats, produce, cheeses, and wine. (Kudler, 2003) For a vision to become smooth, you all must work together as a team and prepare food safely without contaminations forthat vision Kudler Fine Foods want as their business motto

According to the Kudler Fine Foods site the end vision is to have business expand for 10- 15 years at the time of retirement. She wants to sell the entire business and not bea part of it again. (Kudler, 2003) As long as she continues her ways she will be in business for years to come.

## Summary

In conclusion, all companies have issues and problems. The problem statement was "What can Kudler Fine Foods do with an organization that is growing but has a small groupof people doing a lot of responsibilities? This problem can be easily resolved by the right approach to the owner of hiring new positions to make the work less on her and others. (Kudler, 2003) The beginning goal is to bring the finest meats to Southern California area and expand. (Kudler, 2003) The final goal is to expand all over California and U.S. until retirement. (Kudler, 2003) Then, let someone else take over fully. (Kudler, 2003)

# CHAPTER 9

## 100 Future Visions

### Introduction

Kudler Fine Foods realized an opportunity for growth within the gourmet realm that can be appreciated by consumers who truly desire quality tasting foods. Kudler is currently operating within the fine food industry but desire to obtain more. Achieving nothing less than the best, Kudler needs to undergo a thorough analysis that would uncover the best transformation that will be aligned with its vision. The culture, organizational structure and leadership that exist within Kudler will be unveiled to emphasize toeveryone the need when moving internationally within Canada.

### Market Needs

The specific marketing needs is enough funding for catering events, food advertisements, mealtimes, hire proper people to create growth in company throughout the world (University of Phoenix, 2006). "Marketing is an organizational function and a set of processes for creating, communicating, and delivering value to customers and for managing customer relationships in ways that benefit the organization and its stakeholders. Marketing affects all individuals, all organizations, all industries, and all countries" (Kerin, 2006, p.22).

## Market Growth

The growth of marketing will come into play from product, place, pricing and promotions depending on how to start a company expanding for years to come. The competition is high when competing with places like Epicurean and Kitcher, the fine food gourmet shops in Canada. The pricing and promotions will have to be solid to compete as well. The founder of this company will have to make a determination on data collected on the most effective place of business and cheapest way possible (University of Phoenix, 2006).

## SWOT Analysis

In order for Kudler Fine Foods to effectively understand the expansion into Canada, a thorough S.W.O.T (strengths, weaknesses, opportunities and threats) analysis needs to occur. A strength that Kudler has is it offers gourmet foods that are of European style and they can always order specialty items for their consumers with ease. Since Kudler is involved in all aspects of the organization, the risk for bottom-up change is minimal. A weakness that the organization can come across is their products and its longevity.

The organization is known to have all the freshest products and although they donate daily to the neighborhood's charities, the cost of keeping stock in both the United States and Canada can be expensive. This sort of organization cultural change will be either environmental or internal starting from the top-down. "Selling products previously offered only at markets and specialty stores coupled with a distinctive and innovative approach to food retailing" (New Food and Drink Reports, 2007). Opportunities for this organization is increasing its clientele, offering products with innovation approaches, and enlarging their territory internationally. Finally, threats such as Whole Foods can be a little overwhelming for Kudler Fine Foods.

## Competition

When moving into Canada, Kudler Fine Foods has to look at their competition and decide if they will be successful in their venture. Some companies that deal in the Canada market for Gourmet Foods are Sunrise Mercantile located in Tatamagouche NS, and Well-Seasoned Gourmet Food Store in Langley, British Columbia. Both companies have physical stores that people can shop in.

With technology the mainstream, the Internet is also a competitor. Two competitors in Canada are Epicurean Foods International in Kitchener, Ontario, and O Gourmet in Montreal, Quebec. According to the Epicurean Foods website they "produce and distribute over 500 of our own unique gourmet foods and gifts." O Gourmet is the same way offering "more than 1000 fine food products from 20 different countries, and ships anywhere in Canada" (O Gourmet, n.d.).

## Product offering/Product definition

Product offering and identification is very important for Kudler Fine Foods. Kulder commits to giving their customers the highest level of customer satisfaction. Kudler offers a variety of products which are fresh, organic and of high quality. They offer these specialty goods to make a special effort to offer a variety to their customers. These products have been selected to satisfy the needs of their customers. It is important for Kudler to offer the right brand, quantity and price to their customers so they can continue to attract their customers.

# Product Identification

Product identification is important for Kudler Fine Foods because their products can connect with the customer. Kulder has committed themselves to deliver the most distinctive, freshestand highest quality of foods to their customers. In order for Kudler to be successful, they must be able to understand the relationships among their customers and their products. The customer's preference and recognition of these products will assist in helping to satisfy their needs. The customers who can identify with these products will create customer loyalty with Kudler. As Kudler identifies these products, they will produce strong customer satisfaction that will result in the success of the business.

# Justification for Choice of Product

The product of Kudler's is wanted and appreciated in their community. Kudler has segmented a market that values health and quality of life. Kudler is able to meet the needs of their customers by delivering fresh upscale food that is reasonably priced and almost individually made for the consumer. This is a combination of niche and customized marketing. As Kotler and Keller state, "In an attractive niche, customers have a distinct set of needs, [and] they will pay a premium to the firm that best satisfies the need," (2006, p. 242). By staying local and attentive to their segmented market, Kudler will remain justified in their products and service of choice. "A company is customerized when it is able to respond to individual customers by customizing its products, services, and messages on a one-to-one basis." (2006, p. 246).

# Conclusion

The basic culture at Kudler Fine Foods is a clear signal that the organizations' attempts to be a leader for a healthier eating lifestyle are prevalent. Kudler Fine Foods carefully chooses all their herbs, spices and produce and ensures its quality. Kudler has done an outstanding job thus far by staying ahead of the times and in the news. Due to the continuous research, Kudler feels best prepared for any and all changes that may occur in any situation. Making the decisions for expansion within Canada would not only benefit KudlerFine Foods but Canada by bringing a new outlook on fresh food.

# CHAPTER 10

## Classic Airlines Marketing Solution

### Introduction

To cope up with the fast-changing commercial airlines industries, Classic Airlines is confronted with delivering greater values to consumers possessing restrained budgets. In the current scenario, dueto the advent of e-commerce, the expenses of travel industries have decreased. Classic Airlines should take advantage of this situation by focusing on enhancing its existing CRM system, taking control of already established techniques and striving to increase customer loyalty by introduction of a planning process which is transparent.

Adopting the 9-step problem-solving model can solve the problem of Classic Airlines. This model has been incorporated successfully by various organizations. The main steps included in this model are problem identification and consequent definition; designing of the end state goals; alternative solutions identification; assessment of alternatives; risk assessment; decision-making; implementation of plan and finally result evaluation. The following paper has been formulated in accordancewith this model to solve the problem of Classic Airlines.

# Problem Identification

With a fleet of 375 jets, which make 2,300 flights to 240 cities per day, Classic Airlines is undoubtedly the fifth largest airline in the world. Its earnings were a whopping $8.7 billion last year. But the past year also saw a decrease of 10% in the share prices of Classic airlines. Consequently, the company is finding it difficult to cope up with the pressure from the media and Wall Street due to which the morale of its employees is falling rapidly. Additionally, the customer confidence is also falling at a rapid rate, which has led to nervousness among the investors. The rising costs have led to a decrease in the number of frequent fliers and the company has also witnessed a decline in its Reward Program. To cope with these marketing challenges, Classic Airlines needs to reach an optimal solution for survival (University of Phoenix, 2007).

## Issues and Opportunities

The main threats to Classic Airlines are rising costs and over expansion. The firm that has a 32,000 strong staff has witnessed 20% decline in flights as well as and its Reward members have reduced to 19%. Such a situation calls for a complete overhaul of the firm (UOP Portal, Classic Airlines). In addition, the board of directors has issued a directive of 15% cost reduction to be achieved in 18 months. This has increased the pressure upon the company leading to the downfall of stock price by 10%. Another setback for the company was the joining of Amanda Miller as the CEO in 2002. This transition has proved to be unlucky for the company as Mrs. Miller gives priority to operational excellence when the current requirement is focus on the customers and continuous improvement to overcome the competitors.

## Stakeholder Groups

"Organizations must connect not just with their consumers but with all the stakeholders, for the people affected by what the company does and how well it performs" (Kerin et al., 2006). Proper marketing planning and implementation is not possible without alignment of stakeholders. As per the requirements of the customers, trade- offs at all levels should be balanced. Conflicting interests may develop in relationships, which need to be properly managed in accordance with innovative improvement techniques. Although the management of Classic Airlines has attempted to maintain efficiency but was unsuccessful as the market response was not good.

If employees are motivated to familiarize themselves with the consumer, they will get a more clear idea about the target market. This necessitates the development of a cross- functional communication network, which will help in improving interactions with the stakeholder. Such a networkwill play a significant role in the improved CRM system.

## Problem Solution

"Marketing is an organizational function and a set of processes for creating, communicating, and delivering value to customers and for managing customer relationships in ways that benefit the organization and its stakeholders" (Kerin et al, 2006, p.8). Thesuccess of marketing in any organization lies in determination of the needs wants and desires of customers. Hence, the first step for Classic Airlines is to identify market segments or groups, which desire the service. Later, specific strategies that cater to budget limitations and exhibit e-commerce abilities should be planned for this group. To combat with pressures arising within the company due to the advent of e-ticketing, cross-functional applications can be adopted. This would help in increasingemployee turnover and in dealing with morale variations.

Classic should put continuous efforts in knowing the needs and wants of customers as in this global economy; industry trends keep changing at a fast pace. Direct communication with the customer is the best way of understanding the customer instead of wasting time and money in Research and Development. "Firms spend billions of dollars annually on marketing and technical research that significantly reduces, but doesn't eliminate, new product failure" (Kerin et al., 2006).

To develop an effective CRM, the company needs to involve its employees in the decision-making process. When employees take the leadership roles, the transformation process becomes much easier, and value is developed. The CRM should also include a continuous improvement plan for revitalizing all including stakeholders, employees, customers and even the board of directors. The internal CRM has to be restructured in such a way that it not only aligns with the customer but is also cross-functional. The existing CRM can be utilized for gathering data about the Rewards Program. This information can be used to make plans for attracting customers. Another alternative for Classic is to enter into alliance with some other airlines. Although the alliance would be costly, the ROI will be beneficial. Some most favorable alliances would be with Latin American or European airlines.

## End State Vision

As mentioned earlier, the need of the hour for Classic Airlines is to develop a strategically sustainable model of marketing. This model should contain an internal communication network as well so that the internal decision makers are constantly updated about the adjustments made. Classic Airlines is required to have a vision, which will enable the firm to move forward. The main goals of the firm should be to lay emphasis on customer requirements, identify criteria for developing market statement, comprehend value drivers, develop retention and give importance to customer feedback. All these goals can easily be achieved if the company develops an Enterprise-Wide Risk Management (EWRM) approach. This philosophy of EWRM will make continuous assessment possible which is an essential requirement for relationship marketing. Both customer focus and risk need to be ideally balanced for optimum growth of the company.

The main reason behind Classic's downfall is focus on efficiency rather than strategic thinking. In fact, the employees should be motivated to maintain a vision that should include both efficiency and strategy. The marketing strategy with its dual qualities of marketability and sustainability should also be capable of making the stakeholders happy. The organization should also keep in mind that the consumers are the pulse of the company and their needs should be constantly evaluated. Thus, an integrated CRM is needed to uplift Classic Airlines, which can only be possible with rigorous efforts combined with productivity.

## Alternative Solutions

To search for alternative solutions, benchmarking is extremely necessary. In this paper we will focus on three airlines namely: United Airlines, Southwest Airlines and GE.

Because of its constant high respect towards customers and employees, Southwest Airlines has been able to break records in February 2009 by showing profitability consecutively for 36 years. Apart from having good relationships with the customer, the success factor of Southwest lies in strong liquidity, growth initiatives based on realistic revenue and fuel hedging. The prime importance given to relationship marketing by the firm has given a boost to the airline industry. Classic Airlines should perfect its CRM system by adopting this consumer-focused philosophy of Southwest.

United Airlines on the other hand, has laid emphasis on sophisticated technology such as DC power outlet ports, in-flight satellite phones, a liberal cell phone policy (on ground), updated entertainment options and in-flight Wi-Fi. The consumers come to know about the affordability and convenience of these services by a website maintained by the firm for customer communication.

The main success factor of GE was cross functionality which, increased profitability due to increase in consumer value. This focus on consumer has enhanced the growth of the company from a mere $12 billion in

1981 to a whooping \$280 billion in 1998. The main philosophy of the firm behind this tremendous achievement was the merger of traditional policies of efficiency with continuous development and assessment of strategy based on target market values. Such adaptability should be adopted by Classic Airlines to keep pace with the evolution within the industry.

## Analysis of Alternatives

An optimal CRM system can be created only by analysis of available alternatives. Classic Airlines need to combine the concepts of cross functionality and consumer focus while developing its marketing plan. Consumer focus should be the prime focus of the company with second importance given to cross functionality.

To implement a sustainable marketing philosophy, this paper highlights the available alternatives for enlightenment. The communication of EWRM approach in a friendly and easily accessible way is very important. It should be communicated along with strategic points related to customer relationship, significance of transparency and retention elements. A balance should be created between performance measures in a continuously changing industry and a marketing plan. Guidelines should be set to ensure that management is putting its best efforts. The employees of Classic Airlines should be made to understand that constant learning and updating of knowledge is required for successful growth.

## Risk Assessment and Mitigation

With changing trend industry, Classic Airlines may be confronted with trade off choices that are not profitable. To prepare the firm for such challenges, implementation of risk management techniques are required. A strong structure can be built by incorporating EWRM.

"Your organization needs an enterprise-wide process to bring risk intobalance as a strategic imperative in a complex and changing world" (DeLoach, pg 1). EWRM helps in creating an environment, which is more unified thereby enabling continuous improvement in the firm.

One of the first phases of EWRM that involves searching for actual sources of value should be managed with a broad outlook. New drivers are often produced by changes, which come as a surprise for the decision makers. Consequently, it is required that the Classic Airlines team should identify prospective power shifts, evaluate risk and classify elements as intangible or tangible. If a valuable source goes unnoticed, it may create an imbalance. Firms must not fear risk and should embrace it, as it is the best strategy. However, risks can be avoided if traditional risk models are shunned, and an inquisitive or proactive approach is adopted.

Classic Airlines has an existing CRM system, which is overefficient to the extent that it is harmful to the company. As a result, loyal customers have decreased along with stock prices. This has affected the other areas as well. The board of directors should be made aware of the decrease in employee morale due to the pressure of lowering costs.

Senior management can communicate the requirement of controlling costs without harming the stakeholder value by developing guidelines for efficiency. Most of the airline's companies are focusing on fuel hedging with the exception of Southwest, which gives prime importance to consumers.

## Classic Airlines should follow Southwest's approach.

"The ability to define a company's future in terms of its opportunities-not to mention its ability to manage its destiny in an uncertain environment-is a powerful driver of share price" (DeLoach, pg 1). The organization should structure risk management in such a way that optimism and realism is achieved. If EWRM is implemented, the obstacles in communication of risk management will be removed. The goals decided by the firm should be in accordance with the customer needs and the changingtrends of the industry.

Employees, who give more importance to the firm than segments, should be given the task of ongoing assessments so that a successful integrated system is achieved.

# Optimal Solution

It is necessary for a new organization to integrate optimal cycles of consumer feedback and balance value building elements. It should also include relationship marketing practices, relative evaluative criteria, retention techniques and target market segment identification. While the management focuses on changing the previous failed system by following some guidelines, the above- mentioned points should be constantly catered to within the CRM system. Besides being supported by the whole organization, customer focused evaluation of the core material is required to design the new CRM system. "CRM strategies are only effective if they deliverpositive outcomes. It is no longer good enough just to say that you are customer focused, but it matters what you do" (Bull, pg 8).

A change in the perspective of Classic Airlines is required to accommodate concepts like prioritization of services for customer satisfaction, continuous assessment of consumer behavior and marketing planning. Such a new Classic Airlines will definitely leadto sustainability and increase in market share. The conventional approach followed AT classic Airlines paid more attention on efficiency and less on consumers.

The improved CRM, as a part of the new marketing plan, will use communication and integration to line up all functionalities. Additionally, management will discover the current risks within the industry as well as transparent responsibilities. The senior management will welcome multilevel input. Earlier this type of accountability did not exist and mindset of all departments needs to be reoriented.

At this point, communication at Classic Airlines will have full focus. "During the transformation the primary task of the leadership team is a clear, consistent, and unambiguous transmission of their vision to others in the organization" (Pyzdek, pg 100).

When CRM will be connected to activity maintenance, all departments will feel this transformation. The change in perspective towards consumers will lead to changes in the employee activity. Such changes need to be tackled with utmost care as they may require some trade-off decisions.

## Implementation

The success of strategic implementation of CRM at Classic Airlines will depend on the way senior management incorporates holistic consumer voice into the present system. The help of expert IT personnel will also be needed for providing guidance to the employeesto follow the pattern of industry success models while reengineering their policies. Information sessions focusing on relationship marketing will help in dealing with the challenge of change resistance. The company should increase the pace of CRM development due to the increasing awareness among consumers with regard to Internet.

"Another implementation issue is that of sourcing. Many organizations have few alternatives but to outsource a significant portion of their CRM solution as they lack the resources to develop CRM software" (Bull, pg 2). Experts of the industry state that themain reasons behind the failure of majority of CRM systems are deviation from customer focus and process conflicts. Classic Airlinesshould be aware of these facts to grow and maintain relationships.

## Evaluation of Results

For long-term sustainable rewards, Classic Airlines needs to adopt a new balanced approach. Outstanding quality levels can be achieved by placing metrics to ensure optimum CRM performance. Display dashboards are effective means of internal communication, which will help the employees to know the status of a project and make adjustments according to the updated information provided.

An important aspect of the scorecard is that it should display transparency with regard to overall stakeholder information, consumer response, internal insight and performance. Senior management should use this scorecard to optimize their performance to achieve the organizational goals. Scorecards keepa check on the staff and helps in their continuous improvement.

The management should pay attention to another essential concept called causation. Results, which are displayed by the scoreboards, are caused by root causes. Root causes of lost rewards members and the remedy of this situation can be extracted from employees by motivating them. Once the causes of the results are identified, ClassicAirlines will be more in control. Scorecards also help in presenting an elaborate view of the structure of events as well as identifying the elements of the organization. The management should ensure that all employees undergo performance assessment with the help of thesescoreboards, which should be present at all levels of the organization.

"These goals must be operationalized by designing metrics to act as surrogates for the goals. Think of the goals themselves as latent or hidden constructs. The objective is to identify observable thingsdirectly related to the goals that can be measured" (Pyzdek, pg 66). Once emphasis is on retention, the focus on over efficiency will automatically be balanced. In order to have a quantitative and qualitative assessment of the target customer, the finance department should display customer net present value, segments and time periods.

The organization should always remember that the customersare the pulse of a company and sustainability, and high value are two principles for retaining customers and employees. The future successful running of Classic Airlines depends upon an integrated CRM inculcated with productivity.

# References

Bull, Christopher. (2003). Strategic Issues in Customer Relationship Management (CRM) Implementation. Business Process Management Journal. Retrieved June 28, 2009 from Emerald.

Byrne, John A. (1998) How Jack Welch Runs GE. Business Week. Retrieved from Businessweek.com June 28, 2009.

Coyles, Stephanie. Gokey, Timothy. C. (2005). Customer Retention is Not enough. Journal of Consumer Marketing. Vol. 22, number 2, pp 101-105. Retrieved June 28, 2009 from Emerald.

DeLoach, James. (2004). The New Risk Imperative-An Enterprise-Wide Approach. Handbook of Business Strategy. Vol. 5, Number 1, pp 29-34. Retrieved June 28, 2009 from Emerald.

Kelly, Gary. C. (2008). Southwest Annual Report-To Our Shareholders. Retrieved June 28, 2009 from Southwest.com

Kerin, Roger A., Hartley, Steven W., Barkowitz, Eric N., Rudelius, William. (2006). Marketing, 8e. New York. New York: The McGraw-Hill Companies.

Pyzdek, Thomas. (2003) The Six Sigma Handbook. McGraw-Hill Companies. New York

Senge, Peter M., (1990). The Fifth Discipline. New York, New York. Bantam Doubleday Dell Publishing Group.

United Airlines. (2009). United Airlines Business Travel Tools-Travel Info on the Go Retrieved June 28, 2009 from Unitedairlines.com

University of Phoenix Simulation Portal (2009). Classic Airlines. rEsource MBA\570 website.

University of Phoenix. (2007). Scenario: Classic Airlines. Retrieved November 11, 2007, from University of Phoenix, Week One, resource. MBA570: Sustainable Customer Relationships.

Epicurean Foods. (2010). EpicureanFoods.com. Retrieved from http:// www.epicureanfoods.com

Kerin, R.A., Hartley, S.W., Berkowitz, E.N., Ru delius, W. (2006) Marketing. [University Of Phoenix Custom Edition e-Text].New York: The McGraw-Hill Companies.

Kotler & Keller. (2006). Marketing Management (12th ed.). New Jersey: Pearson-Prentice Hall.

New Food and Drinks Report. (Nov 2007).

www.http//globalbusinessinsights.com.ezproxy.apollolibrary.com.rbi/ content/rbi,

Retrieved from University of Phoenix Library

O Gourmet (n.d.) O Gourmet fine food store. Retrieved from http://www.ogourmet.com/

Sunrise Mercantile Gourmet Foods (n.d.) Gourmet Foods Online Store & Gourmet Food Recipes. Retrieved fromhttp://www.sunmerc.com

Well Seasoned. (2006). Well Seasoned - A Gourmet Food Store. Retrieved from http://www.wellseasoned.ca

Glaid, T. Dr. (2009) Week Three Lecture Kudler, K. (2003) Kudler Fine Foods
Kotter, J.P. (1996), Leading Change, Boston, MA: Harvard Business School Press

Banham C. H. (2002), Organisational Change in Small an Medium Sized Enterprises- A Regional Study

Bauer T., Erdogan B. (2010), Organizational Behavior University of Phoenix, (2009), Individual Assignment Apollo Group, (2007) Kudler Fine Foods
https://ecampus.phoenix.edu/secure/aapd/CIST/VOP/Business/Kudler/Internet/KudlerPort.htm

**An Empirical Review of the Stadium Novelty Effect**
Howard, Dennis & Crompton, John (2003). Sports Marketing Quarterly. Volume 12, Number 2:111-117, 2003

**NFL Teams Profiting from New Venues, By:** Morell, John, Amusement Business, 00032344, 05/21/2001, Vol. 113, Issue 20

**Oklahoma City Convention and Visitors Bureau Website**

**Are Public Policies Needed To Level the Playing Field between Cities and Teams**
Rosentraub, Mark S. (1999) Journal of Urban Affairs; Dec99, Vol. 21 Issue 4, p377,19p

**Cities, Sports, and Economic Change: A Retrospective Assessment**
Rosentraub, M.S. (2002) Journal of Urban Affairs; Dec2002, Vol. 24 Issue 5, p549, 15p

**Tourism, Sports and the Centrality of Cities**
Turner, R.S., Rosentraub, M.S. Journal of Urban Affairs; Dec2002, Vol. 24 Issue 5, p487, 6p

**The Impact of Stadiums and Professional Sports on Metropolitan**
Baade, Robert A. Growth and Change, Spring 1990, Vol 21 Issue 2, pl, 14p, 4

**Stadiums and Urban Space**
Rosentraub, Mark S., Sports, Jobs and Taxes: the economic impact of sports teams and stadiums; Washington, D.C. Brookings Institution Press 1997

**The Employment Effect of Teams and Sports Facilities**
Baade, Robert A., Sanderson, Allen R., Sports, Jobs and Taxes: the economic impact of sports teams and stadiums; Washington, D.C. Brookings Institution Press 1997

The National Road- Fort Necessity NB, March 28, 2003, http://www.nps.gov/fone/natlroad.htm

Milestone Historic Document – The Whiskey Rebellion http://www.earlyamerica.com/earlyamerica/milestones/whiskey/

**2000 Pennsylvania Abstract, 2000 Preliminary Population Projections, 1990,**
http://pasdc.hbg.psu.edu/pasdc/Data & Information Data/228a. html

**University of Texas Southwestern Medical Center at Dallas, 2003,**
http://www8.utsouthwestern.edu/utsw/cda/debt48950/files/54147.html

**Pennsylvania Labor Market Information Database System, 2000,**
http://www.palmids.state.pa.us/INCOME.asp?geo

**Pennsylvania Labor Market Information Database System, 2000,** http://www.palmids.state.pa.us/POPULAT.asp?geo

**Pittsburgh Business Times, August 28, 2003**, http://pittsburgh. bizjournals.com/pittsburgh/stories/2003/08/25/daily12.html

www.ingramcontent.com/pod-product-compliance
Lightning Source LLC
Chambersburg PA
CBHW071404050426
42335CB00063B/1633